Understanding
How School Change
Really Happens

Understanding
How School Change
Really Happens

Reform at Brookville High

Rosetta Marantz Cohen

CORWIN PRESS, INC.
A Sage Publications Company
Thousand Oaks, California

For information address:

Corwin Press, Inc.
A Sage Publications Company
2455 Teller Road
Thousand Oaks, California 91320

SAGE Publications Ltd.
6 Bonhill Street
London EC2A 4PU
United Kingdom

SAGE Publications India Pvt. Ltd.
M-32 Market
Greater Kailash I
New Delhi 110 048 India

Printed in the United States of America

Library of Congress Cataloging-in-Publication Data

Cohen, Rosetta Marantz.
    Understanding how school change really happens: reform at
Brookville High / Rosetta Marantz Cohen.
        p.   cm.
    Includes bibliographical references (pp. 141-144) and index.
    ISBN 0-8039-6254-1 (alk. paper).—ISBN 0-8039-6255-X (pbk.:
alk. paper)
        1. School improvement programs—Massachusetts—Case studies.
    2. High schools—Massachusetts—Administration—Case studies.
    3. Teaching teams—Massachusetts—Case studies.
    4. Interdisciplinary approach in education—Massachusetts—Case
studies.   I. Title.
LB2822.83.M4C64   1995
373'.12'009744—dc20   95-22652

This book is printed on acid-free paper.

95 96 97 98 99   10 9 8 7 6 5 4 3 2 1

Corwin Press Project Editor: Susan McElroy
Corwin Press Typesetter: Andrea D. Swanson

Contents

Part 2. Reform in Perspective

Preface

Not every story has a beginning, a middle, and an ending. Stories based on true events, for example, continue on long after the author has set down the pen. For the writer, the ongoing aspect of a story—and the changing nature of its truth—is both a mystery and a frustration. At what point does one say, "I will end here"?

The story of school reform presented in this book has continued after the last researcher taped her last interview in 1993. The leaders of the reform initiative at Brookville High School have continued to struggle for change and have continued to make slow progress in that struggle. Other teachers have joined in the effort. The community has slowly begun to turn its support to the idea of restructuring. Although no dramatic transformations have taken place, a general feeling of sympathy for school change has gradually insinuated itself into the school and town culture. The local paper now publishes human interest stories on promising programs at the high school, and a new school committee has brought an attitude of tolerance to change initiatives. Perhaps most important, people from all constituencies have come to marvel at the dedication and persistence of the teachers who lead the reform effort. Those teachers continue, after 6 years, to work heroically—often against the same odds that inhibited their work in the beginning.

The focus of this story, however, is on the first 3 years of school reform. I choose to write about those first years because they are clearly the most difficult ones for an institution embarking on long-term change initiatives. Also, that difficulty has not been sufficiently documented in the literature on school change. As I assert in the introduction of this book and again in its conclusion, the ordeals experienced by Brookville High in its efforts to remake itself are not unique. They are, I contend, endemic to the relationship between schools and communities in America in the 1990s.

The story of the Quest Program at Brookville High began in 1990, when the recession in Massachusetts was at its height. At that time, when money was in such short supply, reformers could console themselves that their failed efforts to make changes were a result of the temporary condition of the economy. Indeed, money played a considerable part in Quest's initial difficulties. However, the economic plight of the public schools has been little effected by the steady economic recovery of the last few years. Recent front page stories in the *New York Times* have reported that, even in the wealthiest districts outside New York City, taxpayers now balk at passing budgets that several years ago would have been easily voted through. In school districts in the state of Connecticut (a state that set itself up in the late 1980s as a model for dramatic increases in teacher salaries), teachers salaries are being whittled away by successive years of minimal pay increases or even give-backs. Money, in short, is not forthcoming. If basic programs and teachers' salaries are at issue with taxpayers, school reform plans will be even harder to fund.

So it is that even though the story of Quest ended in 1993, the factors that influenced its struggle are ongoing.

ROSETTA MARANTZ COHEN

Acknowledgments

There are many people to whom I am indebted for their help and support in writing this book. Suzannah Wolk, my graduate student and research companion, provided excellent insights and scrupulous field notes. Laura Wenk, a great teacher and friend, also provided ongoing commentary on this project from the much-needed practitioner's perspective. I am also deeply indebted to the teachers of Quest, devoted professionals who tolerated the endless stream of observers and researchers, and who also gave richly of their time in interviews. To Lawrence Fink, Al Rudnitsky, and other colleagues who read the manuscript and offered valuable feedback, sincere thanks. I am very grateful to my editor, Alice Foster, who understood from the start the value of Quest's story. Finally, love and thanks to Sam Scheer, for his extraordinarily discerning eye.

About the Author

Rosetta Marantz Cohen received her bachelor's degree in English from Yale University and her Ed.D. from Teachers College, Columbia University. She taught for 6 years in New York City high schools and is presently Assistant Professor in the Department of Education and Child Study at Smith College. She is the author of *A Lifetime of Teaching* (1991) and *Teaching Through Stories* (in press, 1996).

To Sam

Introduction

All happy families are the same, wrote Tolstoy. Each unhappy family is unhappy in a different way. Tolstoy's words may hold true for the institution of the family, but for the institution of the school the inverse seems to apply: Happy schools—good and productive ones—can be vastly dissimilar to one another. *Goodness,* as Sara Lawrence Lightfoot (1983) has pointed out, comes in all styles and ideologies: It is relative to a school's age and history, to the constituency the school serves, and to the school's professed goals. A good high school in San Antonio, Texas, may bear little resemblance to one in Scarsdale, New York, or Lawrence, Kansas. Local norms and values, budgets, and priorities all influence the look and feel of a well-run institution.

Unhappy schools, on the other hand, are often unhappy in similar ways. Common traits emerge again and again among troubled institutions, whether they are urban or rural, big or small. Some of those commonalities have become part of our daily vocabulary for public schooling: insufficient funding, weak community commitment, lack of clarity and consensus on goals, and poor leadership. These are the big, visible symptoms, and it may be argued that they draw all declining schools into their unhappy kinship.

Perhaps it is because these common symptoms loom so large that school reformers in the 1960s and early 1970s sought to change schools through generic, prescriptive programs. With such dramatic difficulties in evidence, it was easy to imagine schools as giant machines, built from the same faulty parts, and responsive to the same remedies. Indeed, the very term *tinkering* (used by John Goodlad, 1990, Albert Shanker, 1990, and so many others to describe the misguided approach to 1980s school reform) suggests that the mechanical metaphor still prevailed, if not consciously, in the minds of many would-be reformers.

In the last 2 decades, however, school improvement literature has devoted itself to replacing the machine metaphor with the metaphor of school as a living being, a complex and protean cultural organism. Part of the campaign to reimagine the school took the form of affirming each school's essential uniqueness, even for the most troubled schools. Since the publication of the RAND Corporation (1977) study, staff developers have tried hard to respond to that claim of uniqueness. Although visible symptoms of distress may be the same, they argue, each school is unlike any other. Generic medicine will fail. Only the school itself knows what it needs. Consequently, the school must heal itself from within—through reflection, dialogue, and specific strategies tailored to its own purposes.

As an ethnography of school change, this book is grounded in a perspective that is both specific and generic at the same time. In one sense, the book tells a singular story of one particular school and its personal struggle to remake itself. It is the story of the Quest Program, a teacher-designed experiment in curricular reform, now being implemented at a suburban Massachusetts high school. In certain respects, the story of Quest's painful birth and precarious early existence is a specific one. As in all true stories, the characters who populate these pages are unique and idiosyncratic. Their conflicts and successes are specific to this site, this curriculum, and these students. But in other, more important ways, the story of Quest is far from unique. Indeed, it is an archetypal tale of how change happens in many high schools in this country, urban or suburban, rich or poor.

What is the nature of this archetypal story? Difficult financial circumstances are certainly a pervasive part of the picture. Even in a middle-class community, funds to support ongoing change are habitually in short supply. Towns and cities that have, for generations, supported public education now habitually defeat their local school referendums with the argument that funding produces no clear and immediate payback. Indeed, the *bottom-line mentality,* spawned in the Reagan years and turned into national education policy by the late 1980s, has crippled school budgets and destroyed teacher morale. Communities already burdened by years of recession and by a decline in real wages contrive absurd strategies for avoiding investment in schools. Regularly, newspapers run lighthearted human interest pieces about towns voting for school referendums through intricate "menu" plans and ending up supporting the purchase of library books, but not the creation of a library or the hiring of a librarian. In a recent such case in Massachusetts, books were stacked in boxes in the library hallway—a "solution" that seemed to alarm surprisingly few taxpayers.

Other archetypal aspects of this story are the interpersonal crises that continuously plague all close-quartered, under-supported, human endeavors. Teachers, heroic in their goals and beleaguered in their circumstances, often simply cannot get along with one another when the tension of innovation is added to the burden of their work. In Rochester, New York, the site of highly publicized reform efforts, much of the hoped-for change finally foundered on what were called "communication problems," a common euphemism for interpersonal wrangling. Disparate personalities, thrust into new and difficult cooperative missions, without support or training in collaboration, necessarily bristle.

Archetypal also are the drudgery, the exhaustion, the conflicts between outsiders and insiders, the confusion over goals, and the adversarial relationships between teachers and parents. These are endemic characteristics of change.

Taken together, then, there is nothing glamorous or even clear-cut about the modest reforms, which emerged over the course of the 3 years of Quest's existence. Though successes have occurred (e.g., teachers becoming renewed and revitalized, students becoming more tolerant of one another), the day-to-day work of reform is still a complex, ambiguous morass of gains and losses, successes and defeats. Change, when it happens at all, happens slowly and incrementally. It follows no a priori plan, emerging instead as a patchwork of theory, personality, and compromise.

Hard, plain truths about school reform, its arduous processes and honest limitations, have traditionally been hard to find in the literature on restructuring and school change. In 1990, when the teachers and consultants in this story began their work on the Quest program, few studies existed documenting in qualitative terms the arduous reality of school change. Those few that we did find were written in the 1970s,[1] and the programs described in this early research seemed to bear little in common with our own "modern" goals and approach to reform. Literature that was closer to our own work—for example, studies from the late 1980s, including the early material issued from the Coalition of Essential Schools— spoke hardly at all of the kinds of problems we were to encounter, or of the plausible solutions to those problems.

The failure to "tell it like it is" is an understandable phenomenon considering who has most frequently done the telling. Traditionally, those who have reported on the fate of reform programs have been outsiders; for example, researchers and consultants with a stake in promoting specific programs. With careers, grant money, and egos invested in the certainty of success, it is easy for such individuals to see and report only the fragile, short-term bloom, and to move on to another site or another program once the flower started to wither. The nomadic existence of school reformers and their rush to publish happy news may be responsible for any number of ideologically fanatical movements that have waxed and waned over the last few decades, from *writing process* to the Effective Schools Movement and Madeline Hunterism (Donovan, 1992; Gursky, 1991; Hunter, 1991).

Even before they had begun to implement their modest changes, the teachers depicted in this book felt the sting of this "good news only" mentality. Struggling in the early phases of their discussions and confronted with a discordant and suspicious faculty, the reform-minded teachers asked a well-known reformer to speak at the school. The presence of so powerful and passionate a celebrity, it was thought, would serve to unify the many factions in the building. The reformer, however, demurred. He could not throw seeds, he explained, on ground that was not fertile. The reality of school reform, however, is that few grounds are truly "fertile," and that if fertility emerges at all, it will happen at an extraordinarily slow rate, most often in the midst of arid soil.

Educational journals are also responsible for the retreat from truth-telling. Many journals understandably prefer reporting happy product over painful process. Tales of slow and ambiguous change lack the glitzy appeal of stories documenting successful programs in simple terms. They are often long and cumbersome tales, difficult to edit down to a journal format. For all their newfound interest in stories and storytelling, the educational establishment still seems largely dead set on articles with traditional formats, which deviate little from the predictable structures of old process-product research. When ethnographic or case study research is reported, it is still often presented without showing the players' sense of tentativeness and uncertainty. Yet, true stories of school change are, by definition, tales of profound uncertainty.

There are signs, however, that the time is right for a different kind of school reform literature. In the last few years, a small number of studies and reports have begun to emerge, speaking with a new candor about the old themes of reform. For the first time, the difficulty, or even the impossibility, of change has been admitted by individuals who had previously been champions of gung-ho restructuring. In his newly skeptical work, *The Predictable Failure of School Reform,* Seymour Sarason (1990) tells of his own recent conversion to morbid truth telling. Sarason describes an encounter with a former student at a conference. The venerable professor found himself reasserting his "belief in the possibility of change" only to wonder later why his public voice never matched his private, pessimistic thoughts. Also, a recent cover story in the *New England Association Report* (Merina, 1993) tells of the failed attempt to implement statewide "portfolio assessment" in Vermont. The article, entitled "When Bad Things Happen to Good Ideas," presents an uncharacteristically candid look at the virtual impossibility of large-scale change. "There are so many initiatives related to restructuring taking place at once," a teacher is quoted as saying, "they're poorly coordinated and the resources we need to make the changes aren't in place. I'm being pulled in all directions" (p. 5). The Coalition of Essential Schools has also recently made available more candid stories of reform efforts bogged down by commonplace problems. An unpublished paper authored by two Coalition ethnographers (Muncey & McQuillan, 1991) was the first widely circulated tale of defeat our struggling group of reformers had ever found. Already mired in our own mistakes and difficulties, we read the study with great avidity. We were so grateful to see our own experiences validated in print.

This book takes one step to further the newfound candor of the very recent reform literature. It draws the reader inside the process of change and allows him or her to watch its complex unfolding. What can we hope to gain from the painful story of one school's experience with reform? I believe there is much to be gained. Once we acknowledge that difficulty is the norm, that most programs do not unfold as planned, and that failure coexists continuously with success, we can begin our work on a level playing field. Principals, teachers, and consultants too often embark on their reform efforts armed only with the outline of the program they hope to implement, and with a general sense of how things should unfold, based on the optimistic literature of school renewal. When pitfalls emerge, when teachers fail to comply, when budgets dry up, or when internecine fighting distracts players from their best efforts, it is surprising and demoralizing. It should be neither. Understanding how school change really happens—in private planning meetings and in the intimacy of classrooms—arms the prospective change agent with a defense against surprise.

Furthermore, I have found that those involved in school reform (whether on the designing or receiving end, or both) have a great desire to not only have their stories told, but also to hear others speak about their own difficult experiences. Indeed, there is something of a "codependent mentality" among survivors of change efforts. At regional and national conferences, after such difficulties are reported, audiences stream up to the podium like so many ancient mariners intent on telling their own desperate tales. We search continuously for stories that affirm our hardship and small triumphs and that reinforce what we already suspect: The task is Herculean.

There is another purpose for telling the story of one school's efforts at reform, and that is to delineate the requirements, both the supports and resources, that are necessary for change to take root in a lasting way. Although some of the difficulty of reform derives from elusive factors (e.g., human nature), other pervasive problems could be resolved by a genuine commitment of money and manpower. As I discuss in the book's conclusion, change agents (especially teachers in site-based initiatives) can often find themselves supported on the shoreline, only to be abandoned midstream. The story of Brookville High School's reform efforts then, is also a call for more generous and energetic support by local, state, and national constituencies who pay lip service to change but do not follow through with funding and other resources.

The Program, the Site, and the Subjects

This story centers around the design and implementation of the Quest Program, a ninth grade interdisciplinary course designed to fulfill requirements for both history and English. Quest began its first year of implementation as a fully integrated, theme-based alternative to the traditional curriculum. Six teachers, representing five different disciplines, team taught the class together in a single room. Students in Quest "unleveled," a difference from other classes. Indeed, the Quest class represented the high school's first major experiment with heterogeneous grouping. Students in Quest worked together in mixed-ability groups of five or six where they developed jointly designed projects. As the story of Quest will make clear, the goals of this alternative class were both cognitive and affective: The designers of Quest hoped to promote critical thinking and high self-esteem in equal measure.

The Quest experiment itself was set in a public high school in the New England town of Brookville, Massachusetts. Like thousands of other suburban schools across America, Brookville High is an institution in flux. Once an enclave for middle- and working-class Whites whose roots in the local community stretched back for generations, the school has, in recent years, accommodated a rapidly changing population, including growing numbers of minority students, students from low-income homes, and students with special needs. As mentioned earlier, money is forever in short supply at Brookville High School. Laboratory equipment is old, there are too few computers, and textbooks are dated. The physical plant of the school has also fallen into disrepair. There are holes in some walls, and virtually every clock in the building reads a different hour. There is much local talk about the problems of the high school, and much speculation about the reasons for the school's decline. However, the talk has largely failed to raise the critical funding needed to improve the institution.

The main characters in this story are the teachers who come together to design and teach the Quest class. In a number of ways, these teachers are unlikely heroes. Virtually all of them are classroom veterans with more than 20 years of experience at the high school and elsewhere. It is one of the truisms of staff development literature that veteran teachers are the hardest nuts to crack. Dan Lortie (1975) calls them "conservative and present-oriented." Champions of the status-quo, they are among the least likely to embrace change or innovation. Indeed, the burden of an aging, immovable faculty is often used as an excuse against reform. Yet, the three most dogged and devoted of the Quest teachers, Bill McFee, Sue Hinks, and Ellie Polaski have between them 75 years of teaching experience. Two of the three initially took on the Quest program as a sixth class without pay, giving up their free periods for daily conferences, and meeting late into the day to design curriculum.

The story of this program began in the summer of 1990, when a group of interested teachers assembled at Blair College to discuss general issues of curriculum. The story traces the vicissitudes of that first year of planning, the collaborative designing of the Quest curriculum, and then the three subsequent years of implementation. Along the way, the narrative illustrates the great range of complex issues confronting all change agents; the shifting power roles, the teacher's relationship with the college, the ebb and flow of administrative support, and the often problematic relations between teachers themselves.

The Theoretical Framework for Quest

The teachers at Brookville High School chose to build the Quest Program around principles laid out by Theodore Sizer's Coalition for Essential Schools at Brown University. Sizer first introduced those ideas in his 1984 groundbreaking work *Horace's Compromise,* a rare book in that it speaks with equal power to a great range of readers, including the academic community, the cynical practitioner, the novice teacher, and the general public. Since its publication, Sizer and the Coalition organization he founded have developed a large network of schools working to adopt his agenda for school change. Their organization disseminates a monthly newsletter, *Horace,* and sends consultants to schools interested in investigating Coalition strategies. Recently, several state departments of education have joined with Professor Sizer and have offered grant money and other assistance to foster change and promote his principles of school restructuring.

Sizer's notion of school change is built on a series of nine principles outlined in Resource E of this book. Briefly, they are principles seeking to transform the student-teacher relationship and thereby promote a deeper engagement on the part of students, including more accountability, and more serious critical thought. Sizer also calls for teachers to become *generalists* so that more meaningful interdisciplinary work can happen in high school classrooms, and he advocates a range of logistical changes (e.g., smaller teacher loads, more teacher planning time, shifts in teacher responsibilities).

Although Professor Sizer's ideas are mentioned numerous times throughout this text, it does not dwell in great detail on the Coalition's agenda. There are several reasons for this. First, the story of Quest is less about the adoption of a particular reform agenda than it is about the *process* of reform itself. Whether the teachers at Brookville had chosen to follow the principles of Mortimer Adler (1982) in his *Paideia Proposal,* or those of the Holmes Group (1990) in their treatise *Tomorrow's Schools,* or any number of other interesting and viable reform programs, is of less consequence than the progress and struggle of implementation itself. Second, although the Coalition literature served as a starting point for the Quest program, the experiment quickly took on a look of its own, a fact that would not surprise anyone with even a passing knowledge of how reform evolves. Many of Sizer's visions for remaking American high schools were simply too ambitious for the modest budgets and entrenched faculty at Brookville. Some of his more modest goals—particularly those associated with specific curriculum strategies—were easier to adopt, and they continue to inform the work of the teachers throughout these first years of Quest. Most frequently, Coalition theories were revised and modulated to fit the needs and personalities of the teachers involved.

Some Thoughts About Method

Part 1 of this book is intended to read not as an academic treatise or a how-to book, but as a cross between case study and storytelling. Much has been written recently about the power of narrative and storytelling in illuminating concepts too complex for quantification. As a teacher of teachers, I have seen firsthand the dramatic impact of case studies and ethnographies on novices hungry for real-life models. Case studies, autobiographies, and even fictional accounts of classrooms draw readers into the world of teaching and schools with a power that is impossible to achieve with a textbook.

For students of school reform, or consultants and teachers considering embarking on reform projects, or general readers interested in the *dynamics* of schools, this book is meant to convey its reality with the vividness of fiction. For the most part, the story of Quest is presented through an *omniscient perspective.* The book has been built from participant observations, documents, interviews, and taped transcripts of meetings and classes gathered over the course of 3 years. These materials provided a wealth of firsthand dialogue from a multitude of perspectives. At times, however, the omniscient voice shifts, and the researcher's first person voice emerges. As a key participant at several points in the Quest story, I found it unwieldy to refer to my own thoughts in third person. Hence, I altered the narrative perspective to include myself.

The Book's Structure

Because every story springs from a particular context or setting, the book begins with a general discussion of the history of Brookville's schools. Gerald Grant (1988) has eloquently argued that the discipline of educational reform is too frequently ahistorical and that, as change agents, we are frightened of the lessons of the past, fearing we will see our present goals reflected in old failures. History, after all, teaches us to be circumspect and to expect that changes will happen slowly, if at all. What champion of a new reform program wants to be reminded of that fact? Another reason for looking deeply into a school's past, of course, is to know the present school better. Knowledge of a school's past can provide an awareness, for example, of stumbling blocks that will *never* be moved, simply because they are endemic to life in a particular community.

Following this historical background, I present the unfolding story of the reform efforts themselves, and specifically the design and implementation of the Quest Program. This narrative section begins in the summer of 1990 and concludes in the fall of 1993, at the start of the third year. Part 2 of the book begins with a chapter analyzing the various players in the reform process: the teachers, the students, the administrators, and the consultants. This chapter closely considers the roles of each constituency, and what was gained and lost in the process of their participation in reform.

The final chapter of the book analyzes the larger lessons learned in the course of reform work, enumerating a series of understandings specific to the ordeal of change in Brookville—but with resonance to all schools undergoing similar reconstruction. This last chapter considers, in light of the story just told, the apparent limits of the possible. It reexamines the roles of the various players in any reform effort and assesses the state of Quest today, 3 years into implementation.

A Final Note

Throughout the story of Quest, and also in the analytical chapters, I have used pseudonyms in place of the real names of the teachers, the school, and the community. I do this, obviously, to protect the privacy of individuals. Although quoted statements and excerpted conversations are presented as they were spoken (edited only for length and fluency), they are obviously partial, parts of longer and more detailed dialogues. In choosing what to put down and what to omit, the ethnographer necessarily filters reality. I believe that this personal slant adds richness to the narrative, and that the story depicts what truly occurred. Nonetheless, the reader should remember that, ultimately, this ethnography is told largely from my own perspective.

Note

1. Several examples of the candid literature found on reform include Cogan (1976), Foley (1976), Kozuch (1979), and Miles (1980).

PART
1

THE STORY OF QUEST

1

Understanding a School's Historical Context

For people and for communities, a rich history can be both an asset and a liability. Literature is full of tales of youthful stars whose adult lives never matched the glory of their past exploits. For such characters, the memory of greatness is less a consolation than a taunt: Remembering only serves as a reminder of one's newly diminished powers. The same is true for towns and for school systems within towns: A glorious history is a burden in troubled times. Few places in the United States can boast of an educational history comparable to that of Brookville. Founded in 1653 when a entrepreneurial Englishman bought land from local area Native Americans, Brookville was already a vibrant commercial center by the time of the Reformation. The Puritan values of hard work and intellectual rigor seem to have been reflected early on in the development of community educational policy. The town's first meetinghouse, built in 1655, became one of the earliest schools in America. Town records show that in 1662, elders hired the first schoolteacher for Brookville—a young man whose responsibilities of teaching basic literacy were formally distinct from those of the local pastor. He presided during the months when planting and other outdoor labor were inhibited by the brutal New England weather. In dark robes, he taught catechisms of Latin declensions and Greek verbs to a class of six or seven boys.

Archives in the local historical society show, beginning in the late 1680s, a steady and deepening commitment to the concept of public education. By the turn of the 18th century, at least three schools existed in what was still a relatively small community. By the mid-18th century, a formal *school committee* had been established, and, records show, debate had occurred over the creation of a school for girls. By 1792—early by any standard—community leaders had voted to allow girls to attend the various public schools in town, even as two female seminaries opened their doors to young women from all around western Massachusetts.

By the turn of the 19th century, Brookville had evidently gained a reputation as the seat of educational innovation and as an affluent town with a progressive tolerance for the new. The Round Hill School (begun by German-trained educators George Bancroft and Joseph Cogswell) opened as an early experiment in enlightenment-based curricular reform. At Round Hill, the classical curriculum was replaced by a broad range of modern subjects, gymnastics in the open air were emphasized, and all forms of corporal punishment were frowned upon. Thirty years later, John Clarke opened a school for the deaf. It was the first school in America to teach oral speech to deaf children. One of the country's first kindergartens was started during the same decade by Samuel Hill, a Froebel enthusiast whose influence was felt for decades in the community schools.

Steady growth and steady commitment to schools characterized the Brookville community into the 20th century. Schools were built, teachers were hired, and new programs were introduced at an extraordinary rate. In the 20th century, Brookville schools continued to lead the way in progressive, proeducational policies. In 1902, a *teacher institute* was formed as a kind of early staff development organization to provide teachers with resources and reading materials on innovative practices. Several years later, electives began to proliferate in high school curricula, and, by 1910, business-track classes outnumbered college-prep classes by 3:1.

The heyday of Brookville High School clearly began in the 1920s, when class sizes burgeoned year by year, extracurricular activities doubled and then tripled in number, and the school seemed to open itself up to the world beyond its walls, creating community-based programming and supporting yearly school trips to Washington, DC. Curriculum seemed to respond quickly to changes in society, easily integrating evolving technology. One year, the science department offered only one advanced course in chemistry. The next year, chemistry and physics were offered, then a course called "Radio and Code," and then one called "Elements of Aeronautics." With the growing course offerings came a burgeoning youthful faculty, many of them male. *The Nesaki* (the yearbook from the twenties, thirties, and forties) showed scores of well-coifed, white boys and girls crowding into club photos. The giant orchestra, the glee club, the Pro Merito Honor Society, the Hi 5 club, and dozens of other groups grew in their membership at what seemed to be an exponential rate. Year after year, school spirit and patriotism were the leitmotifs of *The Nesaki*. The margins of its pages were filled with American flags and pictures of the Constitution and the Statue of Liberty, and its dedications rang with a kind of rousing, hyperbolic patriotism characteristic of the young in happy and affluent times.

In 1940, the high school was moved into a beautiful new building, a half a mile from the town's center. The block-long, three-story edifice was decorated with Art Deco pilasters and boasted a large gym, a state-of-the-art laboratory, and a lovely stage. Long stretches of playing fields backed the building, so that students no longer were obliged to walk to local parks for competitive sports. Between 1940 and 1960, enrollments remained relatively stable with just under 700 students and a teacher-student ratio of approximately 15:1.

As baby boomers made their way into adolescence, the 20-year-old building began to feel cramped. In the fall of 1960, 839 students were enrolled, and subsequent years' classes promised to be equally large. The large numbers were putting a real strain not only on the high school's facilities but also, according to the parents, on the quality of programs. The community's first response was to institute double sessions and then triple sessions. Arguments over space and community resistance to large-scale renovation of the building led to the resignation of one principal and one superintendent. Finally, in 1965, a new addition was built.

The relationship between school and community seemed somehow changed in the course of the 5-year renovation battle. No longer was it a given that local taxpayers would support the changing needs of the school. Although the booster club still found support among the local merchants and residents still packed the bleachers for football and baseball games, a new adversarial relationship had been born between tax payers and school personnel. As the sixties moved into the seventies, that relationship showed strain in increasingly visible ways. The town itself had begun to change in ways that frightened longtime residents. Situated at the intersection of five colleges (two of them women's colleges), Brookville was fast gaining the national reputation of a left-wing political haven and a refuge for the disenchanted lesbians and Vietnam veterans who arrived in growing numbers as word of the tolerant atmosphere spread. At the high school, the students' rights movement, the reverberations of the Vietnam War, and, to a lesser extent, the Civil Rights movement all served to replace "school spirit" with a spirit of individualism and value relativism. Yearbooks of that period sported no cheerful maxims or rousing statements from the senior class. Indeed, there seemed to be little consensus among the students about what the school should stand for or about what the students' efforts and accomplishments might represent in the larger scheme of things. In the early seventies, some of the yearbooks were stripped of language altogether: There were no dedications, the photographs lacked captions, and the graduating seniors were left nameless in the back of the book, as if any attempt at naming anything would represent an imposition of values. The school, however, still flourished as an academic institution. Not yet abandoned by the local college community, an impressive number of merit scholars still graduated each year, and academic classes (especially those in the honors track) were considered rigorous. Ironically, a school that had once weighted its curriculum in favor of noncollege-prep classes now seemed to direct increasing energies only to that college-bound fraction of the population.

From the 1980s on, Brookville's decline was a familiar story, one that was seemingly reenacted in thousands of middle-class communities around America. First, the school's student population began to grow more heterogeneous. In 1980, 5.3% of the high school student body was nonwhite. By 1989, that number had risen to more than 14%. Most welcomed the changing nature of the population. However, the change required the school to rethink not only its curriculum but also its priorities in terms of the allocation of funds. Massachusetts Proposition 2.5 brought devastating changes to Brookville. This new piece of state legislation placed a mandated ceiling on school-directed tax revenues and cut sharply into school programs, especially those for the disadvantaged and non-English speaking. Space problems were compounded by poor upkeep and maintenance of the building. Without sufficient funds, classrooms fell into alarming disrepair. As often happens, the physical neglect led to a deterioration of morale. Some of the school's most veteran and most venerable teachers retired, and their positions were either left vacant or filled by part-timers whose commitment to the school was necessarily limited. In the fall of 1988, teachers found anti-Semitic and racist graffiti in a bathroom. A new, young teacher named Brenda Grody organized a "Day of Dialogue" wherein classes were suspended for several periods so that teachers and students could talk about the conditions in the school and the growing atmosphere of intolerance. But some veteran teachers felt resentful and manipulated by the program. Many claimed to see little evidence of real racism in the school, calling Brenda's program an example of yet another time-wasting retreat from classwork. "Everything comes at the expense of academics," said one veteran teacher renowned for her high standards. Indeed, as the eighties ended, the faculty at the high school seemed to polarize. Older, veteran teachers (many born and raised within the Brookville community itself) set themselves apart from "the new interlopers" (the young, change-oriented outsiders). In point of fact, the two groups reflected the bifurcated community itself, where five- and six-generation working-class families cohabited uneasily with the more recent residents who were mostly liberal, feminist, and middle class. Faculty meetings became forums for arguments between the two groups. Each group blamed the other for the lower standards that seemed to prevail throughout the school. Veteran teachers would invariably become infuriated by criticisms from the younger teachers, whom they perceived as having little understanding of the traditions binding the school to the community.

The town, once so ardent in its support, now also seemed intent on finding every manner of fault with the high school. Overrides of Proposition 2.5 were defeated as politicians accused school administrators of wastefulness. The superintendent's $70,000 salary was published in the local paper as evidence of pork barreling, and an embarrassing public argument ensued. Local reporters focused on falling test scores and often cited national educational reports published in the mid-1980s as standards against which the local school should be measured. Invariably, it came up short.

In the early 1990s, three reports were released concerning the conditions of the high school. One was the work of an outside consultant, one came from district superintendent Cara Miller, and the third was the school accreditation report from the New England Association of Schools and Colleges. All three reports painted a picture of a school in trouble, and all three overlapped in virtually all of their recommendations.

The New England Association's (1990) report was the most specific. More than 45 recommendations for change were directed at the school's physical plant alone. The mandates ranged from improving the antiquated electrical system to adding doors to lavatory stalls and to properly ventilating the science laboratories. The report unearthed problems that were so ubiquitous that the faculty had stopped seeing them: few classrooms had clocks that worked; poor drainage in the front of the building made for giant sloshy pools each winter; computer downtime seriously inhibited use of the writing lab. In the area of "school climate," the committee noted with diplomacy that multiple problems had resulted in a variety of concerns shared by the professional staff. These problems included changes in personnel at the administrative level, corresponding changes in directives, and unresolved past issues involving students-at-risk, cultural awareness, and ethnic diversity. The report noted that these problems needed to be addressed in an ongoing manner in order to develop a feeling of mutual trust. Finally, the report addressed the area of curriculum and instruction. The findings were painfully accurate:

> The academic program at Brookville High School meets the needs of the academically gifted and college bound students. The number of advanced placement courses and levels supports the most talented of the students. Additionally, students are afforded the opportunity to attend classes at Blair College. The percentage of students who are not college bound or who will be attending technical training post graduate programs are not equally served. Although these students are offered the same number of courses for the core curriculum, there are limited elective offerings. The work-study program, a viable option for some of these students, is not a reliable option which can be used to gain skills necessary for entry level positions after graduation. Nor are the work-bound pupils encouraged to participate in opportunities at Blair College. Work bound students are not equally served by the curriculum.
>
> There is concern among faculty that the courses, which all pupils are required to take, but not required to pass, no longer meet the needs of the high school population. Discussion continues on the need to substitute computer literacy for typing, and critical thinking for speech. . . .
>
> By definition a comprehensive high school must meet the needs of all its pupils and incorporate into its curriculum that concept. Staff and administration must design programs that will provide job entry skills and in-depth occupational training, targeting the non-college, career-oriented pupil.
>
> The different departments within the high school rarely meet with each other. This lack of communication promotes the absence of interdisciplinary activities. A lack of effective communication exists among the curriculum coordinators, among the coordinators and the principal, the principal and the associate superintendent, and the principal and the superintendent. This especially revolves around curriculum issues. . . .

Scheduling is a serious issue. Again, the lack of effective communication surfaces. Although the framework for communication exists, consensus is not achieved. Although coordinators and guidance counselors express a strong desire to help solve the problems, they are not actively involved in the process. (New England Association of Schools and Colleges, 1990, pp. 14-15)

The superintendent's report (itself a litany of problems) concluded with a list of six goals for the high school:

1. Effecting key educational reforms in the areas of curriculum, technology, and restructuring
2. Responding to changing family needs
3. Strengthening parental involvement
4. Advancing and building partnerships
5. Enhancing/expanding resources
6. Improving communication between the schools and the community

The superintendent acknowledged, however, the difficulty of making lasting changes in any of these areas at a time when budgets were being cut and personnel reduced.

In the fall of 1990, the superintendent (Cara Miller) chose to focus her energies on the issue of tracking, possibly partly because it could be addressed the most inexpensively. Herself an advocate of heterogeneous grouping, Miller used the criticisms of the New England Association as a justification for a serious reconsideration of the high school's elaborate leveling system. Leveling at Brookville had come under attack dozens of times in the past, with students and parents criticizing the five-tier system as unfair for those students in the lower tracks.

In November of 1978, a particularly nasty confrontation over the issue erupted when students published an article in the school paper accusing the school of *classism* (i.e., of shunting economically disadvantaged youths into the level three and four classes, and then forgetting about them). The story hit the local paper, and loud defenses were launched by the principal and the superintendent.

Since the late 1970s, attitudes toward tracking at Brookville have fallen over predictable lines. Parents of honors and level one students (who were often among the most vocal and influential adults in the community) fought to retain the system, which they perceived as favoring their children.

Reform-minded administrators and those who had children in lower tracks sought to undo the leveling. Teachers at Brookville were generally split across political lines. The old guard defended the system as better both for themselves and for students. The new, liberal contingent spoke of the "inequality and racism" at the heart of any tracking system. In general, they used the same arguments put forth by the students in the 1970s.

So, in 1990, the new superintendent talked of leveling as a key issue in the high school. At school committee meetings and in public forums about the high school, she expressed again and again her concern over "the excessive divisions between kids." Schooled in the contemporary theories of staff development, however, she stopped short of simply mandating the restructuring of the tracking system. Instead, an "investigatory" team of teachers, parents, and administrators were assigned to gather data on the subject. The very existence of the group and its assigned task elicited skepticism, fear, and resentment from a great range of individuals—particularly those intent on retaining the present system.

Weighted with supporters of heterogeneous grouping, the committee brought to its final session "documented proof" that an unleveled system was superior to a leveled one. An argument ensued, in which each side accused the other of slander, racism, and other crimes. The local newspaper covered the conflict in painful detail, and the meeting ended with no decisions being made at the high school. The paper reported that the committee would continue its investigations next year.

The fact that no decision was reached appeared to many as a worse conclusion than either of the two alternatives (i.e., homogeneous or heterogeneous grouping). For as long as many could remember, the school committee, the administration, and the teachers had found it impossible to come to consensus on anything at all. Task forces and work groups had been routinely formed to address any number of problems (e.g., space problems, discipline problems, morale problems), opinions had been exchanged, and then, invariably, nothing had come of it. A kind of sleepy cynicism had settled on both decision-makers and students alike. "We're like a boat that's drifting and drifting without a rudder or a compass," one teacher aptly put it. "Every once in a while somebody takes out an oar. But you can't get far with an oar—especially if you don't know which direction you're going in."

It is at this point, and in this state, that the story of Quest begins.

2

Planning for Change

On an evening in early July, a group of teachers assembled in the lounge of Morgan Hall, the three-story house that serves as the education building at Blair College. The day had been scorching, and now the warm wet air made the leather lounge couches feel sticky and uncomfortable. The French doors of the lounge had been flung open, and against the low windows a small table bore cookies, cheese, wine, and punch. This was the first formal meeting of the newly formed Blair College/Brookville High School Study Group, and the turnout was vaguely disappointing to the two Blair professors who had agreed to serve as facilitators. Although the superintendent had promised a "large and enthusiastic turnout," only 12 faculty members were present. Two math teachers sat together in an overstuffed chair, leafing through a copy of the *Chronicle of Higher Education*. Four members of the English department had come and were seated at far ends of the room. Two of the four were well-known as ideological enemies, and their presence together at a social engagement like this felt strange and a bit dangerous. Sam (the much-respected shop teacher) had come, as had Jane and Ellie (two Spanish teachers) and a new teacher of biology. All four sat together on the couch with their arms folded against their chests. The special education teacher stood on the outside of the group leaning against the door frame. No administrators were present.

The assembled participants were attending for a variety of reasons. The superintendent, newly interested in establishing partnerships with local colleges, had offered course credit and release time "to all those faithfully attending all study group sessions at Blair College." Steven (the English teacher) suspected that Kay (his colleague) had come as a kind of spy, intent on bringing back to other conservative faculty details of any innovations hatched in the group. Jan (the union representative) had come in part to ensure that nothing happened that might compromise the union's regulations.

On a number of laps sat copies of the "summer reading" for the group: Boyer's (1983) *High School* and Theodore Sizer's (1984) *Horace's Compromise*. The previous spring, a small delegation of teachers had chosen Boyer's book to serve as a "common starting point in discussing innovation." The superintendent and principal had attended a daylong meeting of Sizer's Coalition of Essential Schools and had suggested that Sizer's book might also be interesting grist for discussion. Two dozen copies of both texts were ordered with central funds and were distributed 2 months earlier. About a dozen copies still sat in a large box in the corner of the room.

Earlier in the afternoon, the two Blair faculty members had sat down to gather their thoughts about the upcoming meeting. As yet, no one had laid out goals for the monthly get-togethers to which they had committed themselves. The role of the college professors was undefined, and both were reticent to impose any agenda on the group. Nonetheless, Ed Smith (a specialist in curriculum who had spent more than 10 years working with the high school in one capacity or another) was skeptical that much could be accomplished without a strong guiding hand. On numerous occasions, Ed had been asked to do in-service work with the teachers, and he had invariably been disappointed by what he viewed as a general lack of follow-through. Ed now feared that the group would leap to develop a massive restructuring plan along the lines of Sizer's model, instead of addressing weaknesses in a more manageable way. Ed believed the best approach would be to work on the *microlevel,* encouraging teachers to make small changes in their individual classrooms. He felt that the school didn't need to make sweeping changes in its structure. Instead, the teachers needed to look at their own teaching and to get beyond the activity level to a place where students could begin to do real critical thinking.

What was not spoken about, however, was the hardship of life at Brookville High School. While the Blair College faculty ate their buffet lunches in the glass-front faculty club overlooking Paradise Pond, the Brookville teachers ate their own bag lunches in the windowless cavern of the teachers' room. The faded halls of the high school were dark and the paint was peeling. Textbooks were dated and computers in short supply. Teachers often taught five large classes of students in rooms without working clocks or proper ventilation. Although the physical plant and poor resources alone could not wholly explain the lethargy in the school, they were certainly factors to be reckoned with. Could one really promote meaningful change—even small, microlevel change—when basic survival needs were still unmet?

* * *

Gail Kean, an English teacher with a strong, competent manner, took charge of the meeting. A natural leader, it was Gail who first responded to the superintendent's offer of a study group and who organized the meeting and ordered the books. Gail was relatively new to the school, the wife of a local doctor, and the mother of two recent high school graduates. As one of the few truly affluent teachers, she felt herself marked as something of an outsider in the school. Nevertheless, Gail believed in reform and felt comfortable taking control of things. Standing in front of the assembled group, she opened the meeting forcefully.

"It seems to me," she began, reading down a list on her yellow pad, "that we need to focus on specific goals to begin working on *now*. And—of course, this is only my idea—but I think we should think about starting small. Maybe we could start with some teams of teachers working on interdisciplinary courses, or maybe a journalism course which blends computers. Or maybe we could think about testing all incoming freshmen in reading, writing, and math, so as to develop an intensive summer remedial program."

Kay (the other female English teacher) interrupted, "Testing is bad." Kay was known as a powerful personality with uncompromisingly high standards. "No more testing. They're already losing too much school time for testing. Everything comes before the work of learning—testing, assemblies, sports activities. Students are legitimately excused from my class for sports practice and for drug programs. It's ridiculous. Then—have you noticed?—they start mowing the lawn right outside our windows the minute the school day begins."

"What does this have to do with Ted Sizer?" asked Sam (the shop teacher). A well-thumbed copy of *Horace's Compromise* sat on his lap. "I read this book. I thought we were going to talk about it." The conversation suddenly shifted away from Kay and Gail, to Sam.

"How about experimenting with the Coalition structure in the summer school?"

"What summer school?"

"Last time we talked about what we don't like in the school. Now let's talk about what we want."

"Look how difficult it is to take a group of kids to the library."

"What I feel strongly about is whether the curriculum is relevant."

The discussion took on the shifting buoyancy of a Chinese kite. Pulled in one direction by a stray remark or suggestion, it floated for a moment or two until it was yanked in a counter direction. Non sequitur followed non sequitur. Finally, with little time remaining, the group decided, almost arbitrarily, that a long-range goal for Brookville High would be the creation of some kind of *school-within-a-school*.

"I like Sizer's ideas too," said Gail, "and we've heard a lot of things tonight that sound just like the problems in Sizer's book. But don't you think we need to start small, to look at what's going on in our own individual classes before we start making big, radical changes?" She seemed to be reading Ed's mind, and he quickly picked up on her cue. "Listen," he said, "there's an excellent article by Walter Doyle [1983], which speaks to a number of curriculum issues raised this evening. Why not read the article for our next meeting, and use it as a springboard for talking about changes in the curriculum?" The group quickly agreed to read the article, and various members even volunteered to prepare individual written assessments of their own department's strengths and weaknesses.

"You don't want to hear mine," someone muttered, causing a ripple of nervous laughter.

"Now, now," Gail said, wagging her finger, "we must try to be optimistic. We have to believe that something good can come out of our work here."

It was after 10:00 p.m. when the last of the teachers left Morgan Hall.

The September Meeting

With the beginning of the school year, the atmosphere at monthly meetings took on a dramatically different cast. Where once there had been an excess of unfocused energy, now there was simply exhaustion. With school in session, the 12 teachers arrived at the September meeting after having taught five classes, having attended department meetings, and having argued with guidance counselors over scheduling. By 8:00 p.m., they sat in Morgan Hall either blank faced or bent over piles of ungraded papers. "Wake me when it's over," one teacher whispered to another, settling deep into the leather couch.

The group had shifted slightly in its membership, but the most polarized players returned for a second round. Kay smiled at me wanly as I entered the lounge.

Gail opened the meeting with her usual enthusiasm, but her powerful voice was edged now with tiredness. She read through the points on her agenda, this time omitting the deferential prefaces. First, she had drafted a letter to the Coalition of Essential Schools asking for more literature about their organization. Second, she had brought an article to share about the *Copernican Plan* (Carroll, 1990), an alternative restructuring technique in which teachers teach two 100-minute classes a day for a period of 3 months. She reported that it was being used in a school in Maryland with mixed results. Finally, the local paper was pushing for a story about the group, and Gail asked what we should tell them.

Right off the bat, the strange, flitting style of discussion began again.

"When are we going to visit some schools?" asked Sam with a set, serious expression on his face. The superintendent had promised to make funds available for teachers to visit successfully restructured schools.

"When are we going to have some speakers from the Coalition of Essential Schools?"

"Why don't we begin with our homework?" said Gail, seeing that her initial agenda had sparked no interest. She had clearly decided a priori to avoid the kind of unfocused banter of the previous meeting. "I trust you have all read the Doyle article. Who has come prepared to present?"

Only Jane (the Spanish teacher) raised her hand. A neatly penned report sat in her lap. She would not present her work, however, unless others in the group did too. A murmur of uncomfortable laughter rose from the ranks.

"Who has read the Doyle article?" Several teachers half raised their hands with the tentativeness of students trying to avoid being called upon. Others simply looked beyond Gail, out the window. It was clear that the article had received little attention from the group. And with the new school year so recently started, it was difficult to blame anyone. Not only was the article long, but its language was fairly complex—hardly the nightstand reading a weary teacher anticipates at the end of a long day.

"Perhaps one of the Blair people could explain it to us," someone proffered.

Ed summarized the main points of the article, and his remarks sparked some discussion from the group. Joseph (the chemistry teacher) had started a new honors program in critical thinking that addressed several of the issues raised in Ed's summary. After he described this, a long silence followed.

"What now?" asked Gail. It was late, and the group seemed comforted to near sleep by Joseph's voice and by the fact that there had been no arguments in the course of the evening. "How do we continue our work on curriculum?"

"How about if at the next meeting we each bring examples of something new and exciting that we do well in our classrooms?" offered Steven, another English teacher with a reputation for innovative, unusual techniques. "And why don't we invite the principal and the superintendent to the meeting. It's embarrassing that we keep them away when they've asked to attend again and again."

The absence of the principal (Ian Fitzgerald) and the superintendent (Cara Miller) had been an unspoken point of concern since the first meeting. Gail and others who had initially planned the study group felt strongly that the presence of "bosses" would inhibit the free flow of ideas. There was a general, low-level sense of paranoia surrounding the two administrators, although neither had ever been anything less than supportive of the group. Indeed, no one in the group could articulate a legitimate reason for excluding the two, especially now that they had begun to talk of curricular changes and schools-within-schools.

"I guess we sort of need them at this point," Brenda smiled, "although I feel somehow like we're giving something up by having them here. It felt powerful to exclude them." The group laughed and nodded.

"It's decided then," said Gail, ignoring the Brenda's comment and the laughter. "We'll invite the administration to the next meeting."

Love From the Coalition

Our meeting in October was preceded by a visit from a team of teachers from a nearby Coalition school in New Hampshire. Through a series of phone calls with Gail, it had been decided that the group needed a shot of adrenaline from an outside source, a school that was "already experiencing success" with the kinds of programs Brookville hoped to implement. A phone call to Ted Sizer produced the name of Clay High School, billed by him as "probably one of the most impressive examples of what a school can do if it decides to make itself over." Clay High School, according to Sizer, was like Brookville in that it too was essentially bankrupt when it began to embark on the change process. Under the leadership of a powerful and charismatic principal (habitually described as "a bear of a man"), Clay managed to remake itself without a penny.

Much had been made in recent weeks of the possibilities of reform on a shoestring. President Bush had asserted that "dollar bills don't educate students." And a flood of recent, much-publicized statistics had showed poor payoff for dollars spent on schools. In fact, spending on education had increased by 33% in the 1980s without making any marked improvement in test scores. A front-page article in the *New York Times* (Chira, 1991) told the stirring story of how a principal had succeeded in transforming his ravaged Baltimore high school into a showcase of high test scores and high self-esteem. "I like to say this about school improvement," the principal is quoted as saying, "design the Cadillac, although you end up buying the Ford."

Intrigued by the success of Clay, the group invited a team of teachers from the school to make an evening presentation. The study group lured an impressive number of their own Brookville High School colleagues to the evening session with promises of not only a stimulating evening but also an open bar and Viennese table. The book-lined reading room of Neilson Memorial Library was packed by the principal, the superintendent, Blair students from a variety of disciplines, and Blair faculty interested in new theories of change.

In so grand a context, and with so great a buildup, the presentation of the five Clay teachers was more than disappointing. Promising to speak about their school's various innovative programs—its cluster teaching, advisory system, community involvement programs, and heterogeneous grouping—the presenters instead formed their bewildered audience into "buzz" groups for the purposes of coming up with "goals for the workshop." Several teachers straggled out or moved to the refreshment table as this exercise began. After questions from the various buzz groups were laboriously transcribed on the backboard, little time remained in the evening session. The rest of it was spent in personal reminiscences by the visitors of the minutiae of their own classrooms and in demoralizing assertions that "nothing can be done without a strong and charismatic leader like our principal." A young Clay math teacher, commiserating with skeptics in the crowd, admitted that he didn't deal particularly well with the nontracked system.

More interesting to the assembled group were the elaborate series of handouts brought by the Clay High School teachers. As the shining light of the Coalition of Essential Schools Organization, Clay had compiled a textbook illustration of all the various documents proposed by the Coalition, including extensive "Essential Questions" for each discipline and each grade level, a fully-articulated philosophy, a performance-based policy for graduation entitled "How to Get Out," and other impressive examples of thoughtful innovation. Throughout much of the presentation, teachers and students leafed through these voluminous pages. There seemed a vast discrepancy between what was on paper and what stood before us in Neilson reading room.

The following evening, 20 teachers, the principal, and the superintendent assembled at Morgan Hall. All the regulars and some of the new faculty had come. They leaned, whispering, against the window sills, drinking punch. An odd, almost daffy cheerfulness seemed to have seized the participants of the group.

"If that's the best that exists, we're going to blow them out of the water!" said Sue, a veteran reading teacher. She moved about the room distributing a xeroxed invitation she had typed up the night before:

Will You Be My Partner?

I would like to team teach with anyone who wants to join me. My certifications are in English and social studies.

The tentative plan is for a class with levels one to three. There would be minimum standards for each level, but there will not be a limit on expectations for any one level. Students in levels two and three can opt for level one work at any time, and level one will have no limits. Students will have the options of expanding study vertically or horizontally and will know that there are numerous challenges and investigations available. It would be possible to use various texts of different reading levels covering the same material. I would share the workload of teaching and also as of coaching the study skills, reading skills, and writing skills pertinent to the course. The content teacher would be expert on the curriculum and would often spend time on the more challenging projects requiring greater expertise.

Sue's appeal sparked sudden and voluble talk. A great blaze of interest in the idea of teaming, in establishing advisories for students, and in merging disciplines seemed to have been ignited by the negative example of the Clay presentation, as well as by the provocative literature they had distributed.

"Right in this room," said Sam, "we've got the talent and experience to put together an amazing interdisciplinary team."

"We could form a separate track in the school—a minischool—where bells could be ignored, and kids could work for hours on a single project."

"We could have students going out into the community and developing projects that help to solve some of the city's problems."

The talk seemed to snowball with enthusiasm. Even the quietest members of the group became excited and joined the conversation.

Cara Miller and Ian Fitzgerald sat on the outskirts of the discussion, following the talk from teacher to teacher. It was known that Miller favored any strategy that might serve to dismantle the leveling system in the school. Consequently, talk of unleveled experimental classes was expected to find encouragement from her camp. Indeed, the very fact of her known support for such changes was seen as a hidden agenda on her part. It was clear from her silence that she was waiting for the group to come up with a plan themselves. Her face was impassive.

Inevitably, however, the group began to turn to the problems of implementation, and Miller was forced to speak.

"Don't worry about money," she said, when the conversation became practical. "We'll find a way. We'll find the money." It was suspected that there were "secret stashes" of funds that were hidden within the yearly budget reports, for example salary lines for personnel who had retired and other mysterious sources of emergency money.

"How about the union?" asked Bill. "We're talking about making some drastic changes in our roles as teachers. How will the union take all this?" The group scanned the Morgan lounge to see that neither Jan nor Kay—two vocal critics of reform—were present in the room.

"Don't worry about the union," said Miller. "I guarantee you we'll find a way around the union."

Her certainty—indeed, her very tone of voice—seemed to have a palpably agitating effect on the group. Other questions began to shoot toward the administrators.

"What will happen to our honors classes? If we agree to take part in this experiment for one year, can we get back our honors classes the following year?"

"And what about the schedule? How can the schedule accommodate the eight or ten teachers who chose to do interdisciplinary work together?"

All eyes turned to Dr. Fitzgerald, who sat with both large palms pressed between his knees. He looked to Miller, and finding no help in her averted face, spoke slowly to the group. "I'll do what I can," he said. "I can't promise anything."

He was clearly less than sanguine about the quick assurances Cara had made. Arms now crossed tightly over his chest, he seemed torn between his boss's enthusiasm and his own practicality. His vaguely ambivalent response to the teacher's question immediately added to the level of tension in the room.

"So are you saying we'll lose our honors classes?" asked Rose (the math teacher).

"You won't lose anything," Miller interjected. "Just don't worry about it. Don't worry about the union, about funding, about losing classes. I personally guarantee you that it will work out. You came here tonight filled with fantastic ideas about a new direction for the school. What I'm saying to you is follow those dreams. Get a curriculum on paper. Don't worry about the nitty-gritty. I'm behind you 100%."

Subdued but still resolved, the group laid out a plan for putting their thoughts on paper and for making an informal presentation about their ideas to the school committee the following month.

"This is suddenly happening so fast!" said someone, and everyone else agreed. None could decide, however, whether the speedy pace was good or bad.

"What happened to the "slow process of reflection" we were supposed to be engaging in?"

"What about our assignments?" asked Steven, holding up the "homework" he had suggested in the previous meeting. Everyone laughed, but no one volunteered to either present or listen. "Hold on to it for extra credit," joked Brenda. The group had clearly moved beyond the point of discussing "the way things were" in their classes. They were focusing now on "the way things might be in the future." It was a major step, this commitment to something new and different.

Later, alone with the Blair faculty, Brenda confided the fears that many seemed to harbor. "The superintendent is too enthusiastic," she said. "It makes me suspicious. It makes me uncomfortable."

*   *   *

"The shit has hit the fan."

Steven cornered me in the lobby of the school the following afternoon. He had a wry, resigned expression on his face, as if to say, "I told you so," or "Here we go again."

Kay, it seems, had gotten wind of the talk the previous evening and argued volubly in the faculty room that Miller was merely using the Coalition group to press through her own agenda. "It's all about doing away with ability grouping," she said. "She's using the language of reform and restructuring, but it's just a transparent attempt to do away with the one remaining thread that ties us to excellence. "Here we are," she told the group, "leaping into changes supposedly of our own design, that are really just part of Cara's master plan."

Kay's call to arms in the morning had led to other growing dissent throughout the course of the day. Bill had an argument with a history teacher in the afternoon, as did Steven and another teacher in his own department.

"You simply can't believe how political this school is," Gail told me. "And it's a shame because the bottom line is that there are real problems that need to be addressed—problems that have nothing to do with tracking or leveling."

The following day, a typed memo appeared in the mailboxes of all Brookville High School faculty.

To the members of the Brookville School Committee:

An administrative plan to change the leveling structure at Brookville High School will shortly be proposed to you. Any suggestion that we, the undersigned faculty of BHS (Brookville High School), aided in its development or even approve of its existence would be untrue. Any attempt to characterize us as teachers who espouse heterogeneous grouping as a general goal for our school would be, at the very least, premature.

Reducing levels as a means of coping with scheduling prob-lems may or may not be a necessity in these lean times. However, the proposed system is as much a response to ideological pressure from other sources as it is an attempt to solve real problems at BHS. In trying to make the high school's classes more heteroge-neous in nature, the proposed plan would actually cause more problems than it would solve. If implemented, it would create the sort of tracking system employed by some prep schools, and would result in unfair rank-in-class comparisons and a great deal of extra work for an already overburdened guidance staff.

The impetus to group classes at the high school more hetero-geneously did not originate with us. Reaction among us to the idea ranges from hostile to sympathetic, but all of us would agree that, at this time, general movement toward heterogeneous grouping would be ill-advised. We simply have not been given anywhere near enough opportunity to debate the issue among ourselves in the context where it belongs, our unique school community.

We are a mature and committed faculty, who believe that our teaching at Brookville High School is a worthwhile, productive enterprise and that no one knows this school, its students, and their problems better than we do. In light of these beliefs, we would like to ask you to reject the proposed new leveling system and, in turn, make a commitment to allowing us, the people who do the job, to identify the real problems at BHS and to recommend and create productive change in the future.

Many of the participants of the study group signed the form placed in their boxes. "We must find a way to make change," they said, "without threatening those who don't want to come along. There's got to be a way to do it."

3

Getting Started

The remainder of the fall and winter meetings were marked by the same tone of tired distraction that had characterized our first September meeting. Like postcards from vacationing relatives, literature from the Coalition began arriving on a regular basis. It was full of interesting and innovative program descriptions that seemed to bear little relation to life at the high school. Representatives from the group visited a number of Coalition schools, bringing back stories of experimental classes, dissent among teachers, divisive factions, and other troubling phenomena.

Then, at the meeting in February, Bill McFee arrived with a legal pad covered with writing. "I have a plan," he said, "just an idea, not really worked out." Bill's style was appealingly humble and low key. He looked down when he spoke, and he rarely countered when someone disagreed with him. His genuine modesty and soft-spoken practicality quickly turned the group to his side. He had replaced Gail as the group's unofficial leader.

All eyes turned to Bill as he began to pass out xeroxes of his handwritten notes and to describe the specifics of an interdisciplinary course he'd envisioned for 50 heterogeneously-grouped ninth graders. The class, he said, might be organized around the theme of "the expert" or what it means to be an expert. Eight teachers would teach in a rotating fashion, advancing or receding according to their areas of expertise. The course would last two

periods and would focus on experiential learning techniques. It would culmi-
nate in a final exhibition similar to the ones described in Sizer's work. Bill had
already identified the teachers who were to participate in this pilot program.
During vacation, he had spoken separately with each one and had found real
enthusiasm for the plan. A long silence followed Bill's presentation.

"I think it's great," said Sue, who had been identified to provide the
reading component of the new class.

"The only thing we're asking for," continued Bill, "is to be released
from our study halls. We'll be taking this on as a sixth class: It's two periods
that will count as one, so releasing us from a duty seems fair."

"Tell that to the union."

"We're going to have to have a concession from the union if this is
going to work at all. Maybe a 1-year grace period to see how things work
out."

"What about scheduling this thing? Won't it be impossibly complicated? Getting all eight teachers free at the same time, and keeping at least
some of our remaining classes for us?"

"That's Ian's and Cara's problem. Cara said not to worry about it."
Another long silence fell on the group. "I think we're moving too fast,"
said Gail. She had gained the reputation over the last few months—now
that Kay and Jan had given up on the meetings—of being the resident
conservative and the skeptic. "What are our motives here? Are they really
to start up a new program? Or, are we doing this to please the superintendent because we sense she wants to see something concrete?"

"If you don't like it, then don't take part." The tone of conversation
lately was uncharacteristically blunt. The months of backtracking and
digressing, and the growing familiarity of the group combined to make the
language of discussion somewhat less than cordial at times. A new kind of
intimacy had begun to evolve: it closely resembled that of a troubled
family. Gail was labeled as skeptical, Bill as wise, and Brenda as overly
idealistic.

"I didn't say I didn't like it," pressed Gail. "I didn't say I didn't want
to take part. I'm just saying that we're leaving a lot of the details up to the
principal and the superintendent, and I am not sure that they're going to
attend to them in a way we're going to like." No one seemed interested in
discussing Gail's fears.

Sue began to speak about a program she had seen at nearby Andover
High School which sounded a great deal like Bill's proposed class. She and
the other teachers who had visited the school were overwhelmed with the
level of inquiry, the sophistication of the interactions, and the enthusiasm

of the students. This program was also invented by teachers, and it didn't seem to affect the leveling arrangement in the school.

"So it seems we can sort of have our cake and eat it too," said Clark, the math teacher who had been concerned at one point with the leveling issue.

"Then it's decided," said Brenda. "Let's figure out how to tell the faculty."

* * *

To: Faculty

From: Essential Schools Study Group

Re: Proposed course for 1991-1992 school year. Please read this proposal sometime before the next faculty meeting so that we may come together to discuss it and consider it thoughtfully.

Approximately 20 teachers have met regularly throughout the last year as the Essential Schools Study Group. They have read and discussed recent publications and research on the restructuring secondary education and have been influenced particularly by the work of Theodore Sizer (founder of the Coalition of Essential Schools based at Brown University). The 20 staff and faculty members have been joined at these meetings by several professors from Blair College department of education.

The following is a summary of a proposed 1-year pilot project that involves a new course, "Learning to Learn." The course would be taught collectively by eight teachers at the high school starting in September 1991. Preparation would begin immediately and extend throughout the summer if needed. We need your support for the course if it is to be a viable offering to next year's incoming ninth graders who are beginning to sign up now for next fall's courses.

Eight teachers—Freeland, Kean, Polaski, Slover, McFee, Bishop, Grody, and Hinks—would collectively plan, organize, and teach the curriculum. Two anchor teachers would assume principal responsibility for students and would insure continuity between the program and staff components of the pilot.

Core teachers would periodically report to the entire Essential Schools Study Group as well as to the faculty at large for review and critiques. In-service credit would continue to be offered to all members of the committee who attend meetings regularly.

The students involved would consist of 30 to 40 freshmen in levels one through three, including a small number of at-risk students. They would meet for a double-period block, perhaps for the third and fourth periods, and would receive elective credit for the pilot course in English, or speech, or both.

The philosophical and educational underpinning of the course would be an emphasis on how to learn and think. The purposes of the year-long pilot are to

- introduce students in the ninth grade to the language, assumptions, perspectives, and principles of major academic disciplines;
- encourage the students to practice skills necessary for content areas;
- achieve greater student accountability for independent learning;
- foster higher expectations of students (e.g., for varied modes of demonstrated mastery of subjects); and
- foster interdisciplinary strategies to promote thinking about connections among disciplines.

Academic disciplines to explore would be: English, science, math, technology, historical thinking, foreign language, performing arts, study skills, writing, and research.

Each teacher, with exception of the two anchors, would teach his or her regular five classes in addition to the equivalent of five weeks (or one eighth) of the pilot course. In addition, the teachers would assist in the pilot project by undertaking tasks, such as helping to articulate the objectives of each of the eight core units; observing and evaluating the progress of the pilot; planning classroom strategies; and coteaching, with the aid of the two anchors, the skills inherent in the discipline each teacher represents. In volunteering to launch this pilot, the respective teachers would be, in essence, taking part in both the preparation and teaching, at least on a part-time basis, of a sixth class. In exchange for assuming this workload, these teachers would not be assigned a study hall duty; nor, they hope, would they have to take on more preparations than three classes for their entire teaching load. The two anchors would teach an additional three classes.

Finally, each teacher in the pilot would serve as an advisor or mentor for approximately five students in the course. In this way, these teachers will be assisting, but not replacing, the students' guidance counselors.

Two weeks later, the newly dubbed "Coalition group" prepared to make their pitch for the new course to the faculty as a whole. Faculty support was imperative, it was decided, if the pilot were to have any chance at all of success. Hasty meetings the previous week with the superintendent and the principal had yielded great enthusiasm from both along with tepid assurances that schedules would be worked out and funds made available for designing the elaborate curriculum.

Realizing that teachers were weary by day's end, and hoping to catch them at their most alert point in the meeting, the group had asked to be put first on the agenda of the faculty meeting. Instead, the Coalition's presentation was last on the list of things to cover. Several lengthy business issues were discussed, then a woman from the special education department spent 45 minutes outlining new regulations for Individual Educational Plans (IEPs). Finally, an hour into the meeting, Bill rose to speak. In a fast, clipped voice now familiar to the study group, he moved through the proposal point by point, stopping only at the very end. "Comments? Questions?" The group braced themselves for a barrage of criticism.

But strangely, delightfully, the reaction of the faculty was quietly positive. A number of teachers offered gratuitous praise to the Coalition group for their initiative and hard work. Others offered reservations, but focused their reservations only on the fear that the pilot faculty would be overworked by six classes. No one questioned the fact that the course would be heterogeneously grouped. No one questioned the request that the group be relieved from their duties in study hall. Indeed, after only a minute or two of discussion of the proposed plan, the faculty became sidetracked by the issue of study halls in general—calling them useless opportunities for students to socialize. The remainder of the meeting was occupied with this digression.

* * *

Designing the Quest Curriculum

In the spring of 1991, 10 days of release time were granted by the superintendent for each of the eight participants in the pilot program. The teachers worked with Blair College faculty and were served elegant lunches on porcelain dishes. It was established that the teachers would use this time to collaboratively and democratically devise the curriculum for the coming year.

Great optimism prevailed as teachers and Blair faculty settled themselves into their seminar chairs on a cold morning in mid-February. Bill, Sam, and Brenda had attended a Coalition workshop on the framework for creating an interdisciplinary course. At the workshop, they had practiced brainstorming key questions, activities, and forms of assessment, and the morning was spent reenacting this exercise, first around a theme of change, and then later around the theme of conflict. Lists of essential questions and activities began to pour from the group, and the four blackboards in the classroom were covered with ideas, observations, and strategies for student activities. By the afternoon, the theme of experts had been abandoned, and it was decided that *change* and *conflict* should be the organizing themes of the course.

"This is incredibly stimulating," said Brenda, and everyone agreed. "This is the first time we have ever been away from the building doing something that is intellectually challenging."

Late in the day, Sam (the shop teacher) suggested that the group list on the blackboard those skills that the students should master by the end of the first year of the program.

Ed interrupted. He questioned Sam's use of the word "skills," worrying aloud whether an initial focus on "skills" might not move our work too far from the kind of learning—learning for meaning—that Quest was meant to provoke. Ed went on to remind the group about the distinction between skills and understandings and to discuss metacognitive knowledge (knowledge of how we learn) and its place in the overall goals for Quest.

A long silence followed, as the teachers wrote down Ed's remarks and then reread them. Gail, who had been serving as scribe for the day, erased the word "skill" on the blackboard and wrote "understanding" instead. Another long silence followed.

"Don't they need facts and skills to get to understandings?" asked Clark. As a math teacher, he liked to see things clearly delineated; the well-marked routes toward abstraction. Gail erased the board again and wrote on a spectrum: Facts—Skills—Understandings—Metacognitive Concepts

"Our time is up," said Brenda, and the group laughed with nervous relief. Indeed, Ed's new, qualifying language had introduced an element of difficulty or uncertainty into the discussion that dampened the mood of the morning.

*   *   *

While the cloud of the unwritten curriculum loomed in the back-ground, the second and third all-day sessions were spent in a fury of logistical considerations. Everyone (except Ed) seemed pleased to be working on a series of tasks that required no higher level cognition. First, and after much debate, the program was named Quest. The name suggested the discovery-learning philosophy at the heart of the program. Second, the population of the class was debated. It was decided that students in all five levels (from honors to resource room) would be invited to participate in the course, but that the guidance department would be asked to exclude any obvious troublemakers. Also established was a more concrete structure on which to hang the theme of change. The students would begin the year by looking at the nature of change in themselves; they would then take one step back to consider change on a neighborhood scale; then, they would consider change on a city-wide scale; and finally they would consider change from the perspective of the earth itself (i.e., geological changes and predictions for the future of the planet).

Much of the talk that took place after the second session was darkened by yet another time-consuming logistical decision. The group had decided to elect *anchor teachers* to serve as key coordinators of the Quest program. These two teachers would do the major grunt work during the course of the year (e.g., the xeroxing, the extra grading, the coordinating of the schedule, and the calling of parents). For their additional efforts, the anchors would be allowed to teach Quest as a fifth, rather than a sixth, class.

From the outset of the elections, it was clear that three teachers were vying for the two available anchor slots—Bill, Gail, and Brenda. A secret ballot was cast, and Bill and Gail were chosen by the group. Brenda fell into a slough of despondancy. "I really think this kind of secret balloting is antithetical to the kind of collegiality we're trying to establish here," she argued. "Besides, it runs counter to the interdisciplinary nature of our work to have two English teachers leading the class. Science is a big part of what we're talking about, and it's wrong that it's not represented formally in the anchor team."

Embarrassed, the other teachers quickly moved on to discuss the kinds of desks to be used in the Quest classroom. "This is wrong. This is wrong," pressed Brenda. "We're trying to redefine how colleagues work together, and they won't even discuss something that is very upsetting to one of the colleagues."

*   *   *

At our March meeting, Brenda's disappointment took a back seat to a larger setback. The superintendent had informed us that two of the eight teachers—Brook (a reading specialist) and Gail (the librarian)—were to be laid off at the end of the year. Demoralized, and with only 2 days of sessions remaining, attention turned finally to the development of the curriculum, and Ed was called upon for help.

Ed's suggestion was to abandon the persistent focus on the big picture, and, instead, to look at how specific lessons could be presented more meaningfully. "Start with the very first unit," he suggested. "What do you want the students to learn? What activities do you want them to engage in?"

"Let's break into groups," said Sam. "Each of us can take a unit and answer those questions together."

"I'll do it," said Sue. She seemed bothered by the presence of the Blair faculty, and sometimes muttered under her breath as one or the other spoke. "But I want to go on record that I think this is a bad idea. How can I design a unit if I don't know what precedes it?"

"Design the first unit," someone said. The statement was said gruffly, and the overall tenor of the discussion was becoming prickly. The designing of the curriculum, postponed so long in favor of easier tasks, had become the source of a low-level dread, like a trip to the dentist or a booster shot.

Lately, it took very little to agitate or demoralize the group. A stray comment or uneasy thought cast a pall on the afternoon work. Indeed, the overall tone of work sessions seemed to vacillate between buoyant hilarity and a kind of quiet unease. Part of the instability of mood seemed to derive from the sense of limited time. There was always too much to get done in too few hours, always an urgent need to finish and move on. Implementation, after all, was set to begin in the fall. That left reams of work to be done in only a couple of sessions.

"I feel so rushed," people said again and again. The phrase became the leitmotif of the work group.

Now, the teachers broke into four groups, moved into adjacent rooms, and set to work. No one had the heart to reconvene at the end of the day, and it was decided that all work would be brought, completed, to the next meeting.

A Crisis of Money and Faith

In terms of the budget, the dismissal of the reading teacher and librarian were the tip of an iceberg. The town, indeed the whole state, seemed to be in the throes of an unprecedented fiscal crisis. Forty-five pink slips were issued in the school district in March, with less than half of their recipients having any chance at all of last-minute rehiring. In Massachusetts, California, Illinois, Georgia, and Pennsylvania, massive school reform efforts were being bogged down by a critical lack of funding. Indeed, within the course of a single week in December, three articles appeared in the Boston Globe describing the reluctance of both government and business to invest a penny more in the state's schools.

Governor Weld's School Reform Bill was made public in the winter of 1991, calling for massive changes in the traditional school system and providing virtually nothing in the way of fiscal support for those changes. In Chicago, lack of funds had stalled the much-touted experiment on parent council governance. Chris Whittle's for-profit schools made headlines in May.

In Brookville, the superintendent searched desperately for additional funds. She appealed to the department chairs, asking them to take on an additional class (thus increasing their loads of one or two classes to three classes). They were unresponsive to the idea. "It's every man for himself," one of the coordinators told me. "If we give in on this, they'll be asking for more soon." This survivalist mentality was shared by others, who taught behind closed doors in order to avoid disciplining any students wandering in the halls during class time. Indeed, morale in the high school was low: A new prank—urinating on the radiators in the boys' room—had caught on in the winter, and the windowless halls of the school stank as the weather warmed. In late April, someone set off a cherry bomb in a toilet, and the smoke and turmoil closed down the school for the day. Several teachers formed an ad hoc committee on discipline and set about investigating how 25 other high schools around the state promoted discipline in their buildings. Brookville, it was found, had the most lenient policy of the group. Late in the spring, the faculty voted to institute a hall-pass system. However, some teachers who had resisted the new system claimed they would not comply.

The teachers involved in Quest began to experience their own unique kind of morale problem. Many spoke of a growing hostility directed toward them by teachers not participating in the reform efforts. In the hall, the cafeteria, and the faculty room, a low-level ridicule became part of their daily routine. "What's for lunch at Blair today?" they would be asked, or "If you think discipline is such a problem, how come you're going off for these Quest planning sessions all the time?"

* * *

Teachers arrived at the fifth planning session in May with reams of paper in their hands. Sample units on the self, the neighborhood, the city, and the world had been roughed out by each member of the team. These were distributed with some enthusiasm at the start of the meeting. Every teacher clearly had a territorial feeling about the work that he or she had done.

"Wait till you see what I came up with for the self unit," said Sue. She was distributing, in addition to her "student learnings and activities" for unit one, a series of icebreaker games she had found in a drawer in her study. One showed a picture of two profiles or a vase; another posited a series of nonsense rhymes that were supposed to reveal to the reader deep clues about his personality. "I think these will be great to use on the first few days of school. We have to start thinking about what we'll be doing from day one." The group leafed through the handouts distractedly.

Ed spoke first. He reminded the group that their goals were to move beyond rote learning and to get students engaged in meaningful work, a point he had made several times in the course of our sessions. Now Ed suggested that the group consider organizing their individual units into a kind of template: Which activities contributed to the knowledge base? to literacy? to metacognitive understandings? With the lists complete, the group might then have a better sense of which activities they wanted to use, and in what order.

The group turned immediately to work on Ed's suggestion with what seemed like a combination of relief (at being given direction) and mild confusion. Again, a familiar, sticky dynamic began to assert itself.

"I think that Gail's activity for the first unit is a good one," said Bill. "Maybe we should begin there."

"What about my handouts?" asked Sue.

"What does either of their work have to do with the essential question?"

"I think I prefer Sue's approach. These kids need to get to know one another and feel comfortable before you begin piling on the work."

The afternoon plodded along in a thick soup of essential questions, themes, and activities. By dusk, the air smelled of sweat. Enormous volumes of paper had been generated, and they lay in scribbled masses on the desks and floor.

"I think I'm going to be ill," said Gail, putting her head on the desk and rolling it back and forth.

"It's awfully hard doing this by consensus."

"We never even got to even look at my stuff," said Clark.

We broke till the following week.

* * *

Ed and I arrived at the final full-day session of the Quest planning group, armed with a framework for assembling the information in each unit. We hoped the structure would help the group focus the work of this last day and give more clarity to a process that had remained, for all of us, largely opaque.

Sample Unit Frame: Neighborhood

Step I: Define the problem.

> e.g., What is a neighborhood? What facets in a neighborhood need to be studied in order to answer that question?

Step II: Define the project.

> e.g., To create "rich" descriptions of a specific neighborhood.

Step III: Figure out a sequence of activities that would develop understandings for completing that project.

> e.g., 1. Understanding: SUBJECTIVITY AND PERSPECTIVE
> Interview three people in your neighborhood for definitions of where they feel that neighborhood begins and ends, and why they think so.

> e.g., 2. Understanding: HOW CITY PLANNERS DEFINE NEIGHBORHOODS
> Bring in an architect to speak about city planning.
> Visit city hall and look at maps which show zoning laws and census and voting boundaries.

> e.g., 3. Understanding: HOW NEIGHBORHOODS CHANGE
> Research turn of the century Brookville. Compare your own neighborhood today with its 90-year-old counterpart.
> Bring in a local historian.

Step IV: Insert content from particular subject areas.

> e.g., For Step III, example 1, in English: Read interviews (e.g., Studs Terkel). Discuss perspective, voice, etc. Discuss interviewing skills.

> e.g., For Step III, example 2, in Math: Use the census and zoning maps as the basis for exercises on population distribution, etc.

> e.g., For Step III, example 3, in History: Read and discuss depictions of 19th century New England.

Step V: Oversee independent and group work on the final project.

Bill, who had been assuming an increasingly central role in decision making, studied the framework briefly and announced that he would take on the job of reorganizing and typing the massive curriculum. "If you'll trust me to do it," he said, "I'll use my discretion and get this all down in a single document."

The group acquiesced with gratitude. The bickering and dissension of the previous meetings had worn us all down, and the prospect of one of our group actually taking on such an enormous task filled us with admiration. Bill's offer also opened up the day's agenda. Now, we could discuss again the kinds of consolingly simple logistical issues that had happily preoccupied the group during our first few sessions together.

The group catalogued its most recent setbacks. Several in the group had confirmation of the fact that they would be losing their honors and advanced placement sections because of their participation in Quest. Others would be obliged to teach five separate preparations.

"It's as if we're being punished for taking part in Quest," someone said.

"I told you so," said Gail, whose cynicism had lately deepened. "And how many of you really think the schedule will work out as it's supposed to? How many of you actually think we're going to have a planning period in common?"

"I wish the teachers could make the schedule," said Sam.

The day ended early, with Bill collecting names and addresses so that the finished curriculum could be sent to our houses in June. No one was willing to commit to a meeting during the summer, not even the Blair faculty. This fact clearly did not bode well for the first days of Quest in September. However, those days seemed a lifetime away from the exhausted perspective of the May afternoon.

4

The Trials of Implementation
Year 1

"I told you so," said Gail, to a circle of dazed, gray faces seated around the worn desks of the newly designated Quest classroom. A week into the school year, the six teachers of the Quest pilot were still in shock over what had become of the schedule. Virtually nothing had emerged as promised. The teachers did not have a planning period in common, nor had they been released from study halls and cafeteria duties. Furthermore, three of the six teachers had scheduling conflicts for one of the two Quest periods. Clark and Brenda were scheduled for first period only; Sue was scheduled for second period only. Only Bill and Gail (the anchors) and Sam (the shop teacher) had both hours of Quest accurately slotted into their schedules. Even the teachers' lunch periods fell at different times.

In the first reeling days of school, the group had been too harried to even formally protest the foul-up. Now, after a week of chaos and disorder, they were finally taking stock of their situation.

"Today," began Brenda, "I was in the middle of explaining to the kids how to set up their folders, and the bell rang. Twenty kids jumped up from their seats and raced out the door. Then, I had to get to my advanced placement biology, so I headed out of there just as Clark was walking in for the second half of Quest. He had no idea what I'd just been saying and no idea what the lesson plan was for the day. So, when the kids got back after break, there was no consistency at all. The folders were left sitting on their desks, half filled out."

Other logistical difficulties compounded the lack of shared planning time and the shock of the schedule. The room to which the 40 freshmen were assigned was large enough to hold 20. The special tables that had been requested had not materialized, and the students sat instead at old, unwieldy desks unsuited to cooperative learning (the strategy that was to be the center-piece of the Quest approach). Finally, it seemed that the middle school's guidance department had ignored the teachers' request to keep the trouble-makers out. Many of the students were clearly chronic misbehavers who openly admitted that they were told the program was a kind of special education experiment. During the rare and brief private moments that the teachers had together—usually after school or during the (5 minute) break between classes—curriculum was never the subject of discussion. Instead, the group found itself doing triage on the most drastic behavioral problems of the day. "What on earth is that child David's problem?" "Did you hear the way Stacy spoke to Anna? I never heard language like that even in the army!"

Virtually nothing was accomplished in the first weeks of class. Students balked at the icebreaker activities, calling them pointless and infan-tile. Brief forays into the introductory unit on the self had met with similar hostility. "What's the point? What's the point?" The question was continu-ously rising up from all corners of the room, as surly "cooperative learning groups" worked on games and activities that indeed bore little relation to the larger themes of the course. Among the teachers, a great phobia seemed to have developed for the hard academic substance of the curriculum. The Quest curriculum, laboriously typed by Bill, sat unopened in the English office. Instead, soft exercise followed soft exercise in a largely discon-nected way, with students growing increasingly rambunctious.

"We know what the problem is," said Gail, "we just can't seem to get past it. We know the class is disconnected. We know we haven't gotten to the meat of the course and the kids can't see yet how all the pieces are supposed to fit together. But the discipline problems just seem to over-whelm us. I can't even think straight with all the noise in the room. And there's the teachers coming in and going out, and there's no time to sit down or even to say, 'so what should we do today?' It's impossible."

Understandably, as the weeks passed, Sam, Brenda, and the other nonanchor teachers played increasingly diminishing roles in the Quest classroom. Bill and Gail, as anchors, seemed to be the only ones with the time (albeit scant) to plan the day's activities and to develop the requisite handouts. During class, Brenda, Clark, Ellie, and Sue invariably stood in the corners of the room, issuing ineffectual reprimands to misbehaving students whose names they barely knew. When admonished by one of these "ancillary" faculty, the students often dismissed or ignored the correction. "You're not the real teacher," a student would say. Or, chinning in the direction of Bill, "I only listen to that one."

Indeed, the levels of insubordination in the Quest classroom increased daily, a phenomenon that seemed somehow linked to Quest's stated mission of empowering the students. From the first day of school, the teachers had stressed to the students that the class would be run as a democracy. All rules would be developed through consensus, as would punishments for infractions of those rules. Students would be invited to help develop curriculum, and their input would be valued in every aspect of the course.

This concern on the teachers' parts for democracy and empowerment had emerged from the reform literature that stood at the heart of Quest— literature stressing mentoring, the development of self-esteem, and respect for individual differences. "All the people in this classroom should have ownership of what goes on here," said Bill when he introduced the concept of democratic rule making. The newly empowered ninth graders went on to design rules with the abandon of puppies let out in the backyard. "We should be allowed to smoke in class!" "Cheaters should be punished by torture and death!" "If we need passes for the boys' room, then teachers have to have them too!" After several days and much commotion, a series of diluted laws and consequences were laid out and then tacked on the bulletin board (e.g., "All students and teachers will respect one another. All teachers and students will bring notebooks and pencils to class.") The ubiquitous punishment for all infractions was the time-out chair, a concept that sat uneasily with students from the start, given that it smacked of their childhoods, and lacked the adult, punitive glamour of a detention or worse.

The democratic rules were ignored from day one. Students called out with equanimity whatever feeling or sensation seemed to momentarily enter their minds: "I don't like that teacher," a student would assert, and Brenda, Sue, Ellie, and Sam would look to one another unsure whether to make an issue of the remark, or whether to accept it as a legitimate expression of personal preference.

As part of the effort to respect student input, Bill and Gail periodically asked students to evaluate the progress of the class. Ten minutes at the start of each week's class would be devoted to answering questions in writing.

1. What is the best thing that happened in class this week?

2. What did you learn about working in groups this week?

3. Is there anything you would like to change about this class?

The discussion that followed these evaluative exercises invariably brought to light basic and painful truths.

"We're treated like babies."

"*Why* are we doing this stuff?"

"Why do we spend so much time talking about stuff and so little time doing anything?"

"Nobody takes this class seriously."

"Why," Bill would ask, "do you think nobody takes this class seriously?"

"Because we're treated like babies."

"Because we don't do anything."

And the talk would continue in circles.

A (Dismal) Day in the Life of Quest, 1991

By October, Bill and Gail managed at last to pull the curriculum back on target. They had outlined for the group the larger themes of Quest: the progression from self to neighborhood to city to world. They had also explained the concept of the *final exhibition,* in which groups of students would be asked to present, in a public forum, a culmination of the year's learning. The final exhibition this year would be the creation of a model city, one which reflected student understandings of real neighborhoods and cities, past and present. Students would design ideal schools, public works, transportation systems, care for the elderly, and so on by drawing from their readings, field trips, and interviews with community officials.

The first step in the year-long progress toward the exhibition was the creation of student teams. These teams, Bill explained, would work together all year long, and team members would be responsible for each other's efforts. The focus of the groups would be on consensus building and teamwork. With that, he broke the 40 students into groups of five or six, and asked them to set about establishing basic information about their hypothetical cities (e.g., the city's name, its population, location, natural resources).

"Once you have established this information," he explained, "you will come before a town board composed of the teachers in this class, and you will be asked to answer questions concerning your preliminary decisions. If everyone in the group can answer all the questions to the satisfaction of the board, you will be granted a town charter, and may proceed with your work."

The first group called to the town board was composed of three boys and two girls. They shuffled to the front of the room to a chorus of hoots and catcalls.

"This is a serious public ceremony," said Gail, but her voice was either unheard or ignored.

"We are here convened," began Bill in a mock-official voice, still partly obscured by the din, "to hear the request of Group One for a city charter. Group One, what do you propose to call yourself?"

David, a dark-haired boy stood up, clutching his ragged notes. "We're going to call our city Sock-one-on-mee."

The class erupted into wild laughter, falling from their seats and banging their fists on the desks.

"That's enough! That's enough!"

"That's inappropriate," said Gail, growing red with anger, "completely, utterly inappropriate."

"You said we could name our town whatever we wanted!"

"Yeah! Yeah!" a chorus of angry affirmation came up from the class.

"Suck-on-mee is completely inappropriate! It's something an 8-year-old would say!"

The class erupted again at Gail's embarrassing misnomer and also at her anger, which the students seemed to take as a direct attack on themselves. Lately, it was Gail who assumed both the brunt of discipline and the brunt of student hostility. The most traditional of all the Quest teachers, she was most deeply and most frequently offended by student remarks and student license.

"I'm outraged and offended by your behavior."

"Get rid of her! Get rid of that one!" The students, in a rising melee, called out to Bill, in whom they saw their greatest ally.

"Guys, please, let's just continue," pleaded Bill.

"We cannot continue until they change the name of their city."

"I don't think we should make a big deal of the name right now."

"Well, I do." With obvious pleasure, the students watched the rising argument between Gail and Bill.

The Clash of Teacher Personalities

With all the scheduling snafus, the student behavior problems, and the efforts to resolve the curriculum, it took several months to acknowledge another painful reality: The teachers, especially the anchor teachers (Bill and

Gail), were profoundly and consistently at odds with one another. In the spring of the previous year, when the many logistical details of Quest were being decided, it had never occurred to any of us to consider the impact of personalities on the dynamics of the classroom. Certainly, nothing in the literature on collaboration had suggested that interpersonal issues would become such an overwhelming preoccupation. In fact, we had found no firsthand accounts of collaborations breaking down from internecine arguments.

Yet at Brookville, from the first days of school, contradiction and dissent seemed to prevail. The difficulties were grounded in two basic realities. The first was that Gail and Bill were essentially incompatible in their philosophies of education. Both were excellent teachers with powerful personalities in their own classrooms. However, their styles and expectations clashed in a common context. Bill's style was laid-back, bantering, and spontaneous. His quick wit let him verbally spar with students in a fashion that never became sarcastic. His pace was slow and meandering, with digressions leading inexorably to a predetermined goal. Gail's style was businesslike and focused. Highly organized and thorough, she prepared scrupulously and felt most comfortable exerting a benign but controlling hand over the class. Her overriding concern was with the acquisition of clear, measurable skills. The fundamental differences between these two individuals came out clearly in interviews conducted in the first week of Quest's implementation. When asked how they hoped to change as a result of the Quest experience, Gail responded that she hoped, "to replenish my bag of tricks for the classroom and to become more educated about issues of restructuring." Bill hoped "for a certain amount of personal growth." When asked where they hoped the students would be 6 months hence, Gail's response clearly reflected her philosophy: "I hope to see skills sharpened, the ability to ask good questions, and more enthusiasm for learning." Bill's answer reflected his philosophy: "I hope to see a spirit of unity among the kids and a sense of ownership of the class."

Differences in ideology like these might, under different circumstances, have made for warm and lively conversation at a dinner party. In the context of a chaotic classroom, with the added elements of exhaustion and frustration, the differences became exaggerated and unbridgeable. Petty disputes over classroom procedure were played out, increasingly in full view of the students who, themselves schooled in the politics of parental dissent, often seemed to exploit the situation for their own gain. When one teacher's instructions were too exacting, students would simply turn to a second teacher, whose response would often, unwittingly, contradict the first. Then the teachers would become angry with one another.

A second factor contributing to the interpersonal morass was a profound confusion by the nonanchor participants over roles. By virtue of their peripheral position in the daily curriculum, Sue, Ellie, Brenda, and Sam wielded little if any real authority in the classroom. Having hardly participated in decisions about class activities, they felt understandably reticent about intervening in disputes over procedure. Indeed, as Bill and Gail became increasingly central players, the other teachers seemed to draw back even in the area of discipline, allowing misbehavior to go on under their noses. "I just don't know what is supposed to be acceptable or unacceptable anymore," said Brenda. "I feel profoundly out of it."

Classroom tensions and confusion persisted through September, October, and November. Blair faculty advanced and retreated at various points throughout the fall, offering advice on curriculum or management issues, then drawing back in a pique when their suggestions were necessarily ignored by the beleaguered teachers. "All your problems are grounded in the fact that the curriculum lacks substance. What happened to the document you wrote last year? Why aren't you using it?" The questioning came up again and again whenever the teachers congregated at Blair. Invariably, Bill and Gail would respond that they were doing the best they could under the circumstances. They would dutifully write down the suggestions proffered by their college collaborators, and then return to the distracting pressures of the Quest classroom. Daily the rift between theory and practice grew painfully more evident. So, too, did the rift between theorists and practitioners, with teachers and Blair faculty growing quietly and inexorably estranged.

Outside the walls of the Quest classroom, other tensions were brewing. Stretched to their limit, the Quest teachers had thought little about the impact of their program on other teachers in the school.

"What's going on in there?" teachers would ask in the faculty room and cafeteria. "We hear noise and lots of movement, but nobody talks about how things are going."

Indeed, two factors seemed to be contributing to the Quest teachers' silence about their program. The first one was depression. "We had such high hopes, and the reality is so demoralizing," said Brenda. "Nothing is working out as planned." The second silencing factor was defensiveness. From the earliest planning days, the Quest teachers had seen themselves as highly vulnerable in the social context of the school. Their enthusiasm for change was vaguely embarrassing, their willingness to take on extra work without compensation was unseemly. Now, as they struggled with implementation, their vulnerability was redoubled. Not only were they overextending themselves and risking loss of face by appearing to be daily brownnosers to the administration, but their best efforts were producing bad results. It was a deeply embarrassing situation, and one which seemed to drive the Quest participants into a kind of hibernation.

The constituency from which they could *not* hide, however, was that of the parents. After an early series of student withdrawals from the Quest program, teachers decided to meet on a regular basis with the parents of the remaining Quest students. Monthly meetings at the school brought large numbers of increasingly concerned mothers and fathers, proffering stories of chaos and distraction.

"What are you going to do about the noise?" parents would ask.

"When is my son going to be reading *The Odyssey* like the other ninth graders?"

"My daughter tells me she does all the work in her city group. The other kids just sit back and socialize."

Bill, Sue, Gail, and the others had originally hoped to use the monthly parent meetings as a forum for discussing the philosophical basis for Quest and the larger goals of the course. Instead, they often found themselves doing damage control—explaining the same things again and again, apologizing, and promising better in the weeks to come.

A Series of Lucky Breaks

"I wake up each morning with dread," said Gail. "I leave the school each day with a migraine. I simply can't continue doing this anymore." In January, Gail stepped down from her role as anchor teacher and was replaced by Sue (the reading teacher). In relinquishing her place as Bill's partner, Gail handed to him the ideological reigns of the program. Gone was the conflict between freedom and control, conservative and liberal. Suddenly, a great knot of tension seemed to be eased. The question of leadership, always ambiguous when two powerful personalities had ruled the class, now seemed clearly resolved: Bill was the head teacher, the key decision maker, and Sue assumed the secondary role as facilitator. A first turbulent marriage had been replaced by a peaceful one built on conventional roles. What is more, the other teachers voluntarily stepped back even further, becoming quiet third wheels and only occasionally coming forward to present information or skills related to their specific disciplines.

As the teaching structure of the class moved away from the innovation of the team approach toward the familiar and conventional, a new calm settled on the Quest classroom. Students began working more comfortably in their groups, still distracted and rambunctious, but with a new good nature both toward one another and toward the teachers. The student teams (or city groups) slowly began to develop a kind of war loyalty among the members, patting each other on the back for the slightest bit of work accomplished, and quoting one another in group discussions. Students came to identify each other's strengths and weaknesses with the sureness of siblings: "David doesn't like to write," Stacy told me of the longhaired boy on her right. I had seen David sitting sullenly alone at the start of the year, his desk pulled against the radiator. Now I leaned over his shoulder. "He prefers to work on the map and do hands-on kinds of things." David smiled at her and nodded in agreement.

Students seemed to turn with relief and gratitude to Bill for establishing what they saw to be a new domestic peace. Their relationship with him—and, to a lesser extent, with the remaining teachers—became one of good-natured familiarity, often bordering on presumptuousness. With Gail more in the background, a spirit of informality and ease, a kind of caricature of Bill's own style, seemed to pervade the room. The students often addressed Bill as "Mack" (Bill's nickname among the faculty). And some of the large, combative boys (e.g., David, Isaac, and Billy) assumed a kind of warm, patronizing pose toward him, putting their arms around his shoulder when he spoke individually to them and patting him on the head. "Mack, my man," Isaac would say, "you're the one I intend to call to bail me out of jail." "I'm deeply flattered," Bill would counter.

Some good luck followed. In their desperation to generate curriculum and to get some of the burden of work off their own backs, the teachers were relying to a growing extent on the visits of outside speakers. Outside speakers required little preparation on the teachers' part except the logistical preparation of telephoning and scheduling—work easily divvied out to others. In the weeks after New Year's Day, a long parade of local lawyers, city officials, archivists, and historians came to the Quest class to lecture on a range of city issues. These visits were spotty in their success: Some speakers spoke far above the students' heads, eliciting loud, humiliating yawns from an audience not trained to repress its true feelings. Other speakers masterfully engaged the students.

As luck would have it, one of the first speakers to be invited was the recently retired city mayor. A former teacher himself, with a penchant for progressive programs and with unaccustomed time on his hands, Mayor Berkley volunteered to attend the Quest class on a regular basis and to serve, as it were, as an on-site, ongoing consultant for the evolving exhibitions (i.e., the work of creating ideal cities). In the months that followed, Berkley brought with him a long series of former associates (councilmen and contractors) who spoke to the students about a range of city issues. Great quantities of information poured into the classroom. However, neither the level of expectation in the classroom, nor the pace of the students' work changed. A spirit of excitement, of "things happening," took hold of teachers and students alike.

On a typical early spring day, a visitor to the Quest classroom would see ragged configurations of teams, with their desks pulled halfheartedly toward one another. Large, sprawling students inhabited those desks, many frequently getting up and moving lackadaisically around the classroom. Spread out across the desks were maps and papers, scissors, tape, old newspaper articles, notebook paper covered with scribbled drafts, candy wrappers, hairbrushes, and other adolescent paraphernalia.

Within the city groups, the students were supposed to be working on a catalog of city projects. Each group was to produce a map, a newspaper, a written history of the city, and a travel brochure outlining the city's virtues, industrial base, and geographical features.

Invariably, one or two students would be bent intensely over a piece of this ongoing exhibition project. Other students would be conversing with one another on a great range of topics, such as the project itself, the basketball game, and the math homework due in the next class. Teachers would meander from group to group, warmly praising the work of the engaged students and mildly coaxing (to no effect) the distracted to work.

Like pets never exposed to a cruel hand, the nonengaged students seemed to feel no fear at all of approaching adults and continued their socializing with alacrity. When a passing grown-up stopped to offer help, students would turn back to their work with good-natured condescension and allow the teacher to do a bit of the abandoned project languishing on the desk. Then, when the adult was finished, the student would calmly turn back to his or her interrupted conversation. Even visiting mayors, college professors, and lawyers whose names were often in the local paper elicited no awe or change of behavior. The peculiar setup of Quest and the values it stressed seemed to create extraordinary self-possession and confidence in its youthful constituency. Among the hard working and the nonengaged students alike, a uniquely democratic vision seemed to have taken hold: Nothing was overly impressive. Entering midclass, a visitor might ask a student to identify the speaker in front of the room. "That? That's some senator," Matt would answer. "He's going to help me with the voting districts on my map."

Within the groups themselves, the students developed tolerance for their dramatic differences in talent and intellect. While parents worried that one or two students were doing all the work, the working students themselves seemed less bothered. Differences were seen as matter-of-fact and a source of neither pride nor shame.

"I do the history," said one student, "because I like to write and I write well. Chris doesn't write well, but he likes to draw. So, Chris does the map. Stacy's doing the newspaper, I think. I haven't seen her for a while."

Students also began to know their evolving cities in ways showing at least a passing commitment to what they were doing. With unique confidence, the students would answer questions about their work posed by a visitor. "Tell me something of the history of your town," I would ask. And the students would come back with an impressive litany of facts and dates: "Questville was founded in 1867 when Elmer and Sadie Tompkins came down from Canada and bought the land from the Indians. Then, in 1890, Elmer Bernstein created the first ski lift, and Questville became a popular center for winter sports." Often the information proffered with such authority had little or no foundation in plausible history. Instead, the groups seemed to work at creating mutual fairy tales, which, once composed, became discussed and defended with great rigor. But the hard historical work that would have transformed the city material into impressive, challenging projects never got done.

The Quest teachers were highly conscious of the dubious rigor of their students' work. In March, several of them spoke with candor about the soft product they saw emerging. "I'm unhappy that we're not getting at the deeper issues with the kids. Our expectations were greater than reality and the reality is they aren't yet doing higher level thinking," said Bill.

Bill, Ellie, Sue, and one or two other teachers had staked out one afternoon a week to sit and assess the class. Ellie agreed with Bill's assessment of the students' skills but placed the blame elsewhere. "I wish we could do more with the curriculum, rather than this piecemeal kind of stuff. But, without common planning time, it's really impossible."

The Final Exhibition

The lethargy that prevailed in the City Groups came to a sudden, screeching halt 3 weeks before the end of the year. For months, teachers had been trying to impress on the Quest students that the exhibition was a *public* display—that the principal, the superintendent, the newspapers, and local officials, along with their parents and teachers, would be in attendance. Moved by the same spirit of democracy that had left them unfazed by their renowned visitors, the students remained unmoved by these exhortations. The pace of work remained slow, and the quality soft.

Bill and Sue agonized over the exhibition. Should they cancel it? Would the quality of the work produced simply serve to undermine the reform efforts in the school? Would the teachers be publicly humiliated?

Then, with the same inexplicable logic that had salvaged Quest from the edge of failure months before, the students began to work with frenzied purpose. "It was as if it finally clicked for them," said Brook, a part-time researcher in the classroom. "They suddenly made the connection between what they were doing in their city groups and the final product they were supposed to produce. It was as if they'd been sleepwalking up to that point, and they suddenly woke up."

Everyone felt the change—the new purposefulness, the clarity of goals. However, no one could explain what had prompted it. During its final 3 weeks, the Quest classroom took on the quality of a medieval guild, with many hands working toward a single end.

"If we could just get the kids to see their work all year as being this intimately connected to the final exhibition, we'd be in business," said Ellie, surveying the intensity and rigor.

At 8:00 a.m. on a Thursday in May, the first Quest exhibition took place. Bedecked in dresses, or sports jackets and ties, the 40 Quest students stood behind table displays of their ideal cities. On the walls behind them hung carefully typed copies of their city newspapers, their travel brochures, and the transcripts of various interviews conducted with city officials. Several of the groups had worked with Bill, an amateur filmmaker, to produce brief videos of their cities. One group had created a Linkway program, using sophisticated graphics to introduce viewers to the various members of their city group. Visitors had been asked to quiz the members of each city group on the specific programs, policies, and geographical features of their cities. "In the spirit of cooperative learning, which stands at the foundation of our work in Quest, we expect that every student will be able to answer questions on every aspect of his or her city, regardless of whether she worked on that aspect or not."

Aside from the Quest faculty, few teachers came to the exhibition, a fact noted with both relief and disappointment. Parents, however, came out in great numbers, moving from group to group in the brightly lit library, quizzing the students and leafing through the materials laid out for display. Student excitement could hardly be contained, as they answered their adult audience with a characteristic combination of earnestness and hubris. Some of the students spoke with great poise and intelligence. Many others spoke with glib illogic, reflecting the months of indifference and distraction.

"What is the primary industry in your town?"

"Skiing. We have tourism from skiing."

"But I notice that your city is off the coast of Florida. Is there any snow?"

"We have water slides in the summer. Ask Sam," the student would laugh, motioning me toward his friend, and turning to a more sympathetic listener.

The evening received mixed reviews. Visitors commented on the group loyalty, the enthusiasm, and the self-confidence of the youthful presenters. "The wonderful sense of togetherness impressed me." "The kids seemed to really feel pride in their work." But the content of the Quest exhibition was less than impressive. The few outside Quest faculty that attended the display spoke to that effect in the faculty lounge the following day, as did the Quest faculty themselves. "We know we have a way to go," said Bill, "especially in terms of the content." His voice betrayed not a bit of defensiveness. The teachers of Quest, like their students, had developed an extraordinary candor about their own strengths and weaknesses as educators. They spoke without flinching about what had been done poorly, and without any particular humility about what had been done well. "We did a lousy job with the research projects," Bill would say. "We were fantastic with the speaking skills."

"Next year, " he continued in the faculty lounge, "we want to really focus on developing the quality of the work. Next year, I would keep the general thrust the way it is. What I would do differently, as soon as we meet those kids in September, is make sure they have the impression that this is serious. That we expect hard work." Ellie echoed Bill's sentiments, "We need to do more in class, challenge the kids more, demand more from them. I really thought we could get more out of them. I thought the class would fly on its own. It doesn't work that way."

Even the most critical of the ancillary Quest faculty, however, had to admit that the success of Quest resided in its affective dimension. Students, representing a vast range of intelligence, personality, and interests, had come to enjoy and respect one another in ways that clearly differed from the norm. "The kids have really bonded with us and with one another," said Sue. "It's an amazing thing to see a kid like Stacy. For heaven's sake, she was on her way to Blair Voc [the local vocational school] when we got her. Now, she's bloomed. I bet she goes to college. She's done some amazing work for us."

Taking Stock

In the middle of June, Bill, Sue, Ellie, Sam, Brenda, and Gail sat together taking stock of "the hardest year of our careers." They spoke of the terrible toll Quest had taken on Bill's health (his back had gone out and his diabetes had worsened). They spoke of the strain of teaching six classes, a strain showing itself on every face. And there were other casualties, beyond the physical. Gail, disenchanted, had decided to leave teaching, at least for a while. Relations with non-Quest faculty had grown steadily cooler. The teachers, burned too many times, had lost faith in their administrators.

And yet, seated together at year's end, all but Gail hoped to take part in some kind of Quest program again. For all five teachers, the collegiality and shared intimacy that had characterized teacher-teacher relations in Quest were ultimately worth the work and worry. "The lack of competition, the freedom to share ideas, the presence of a shoulder to lean on—I don't know how I lived without them before," said Ellie. And the sentiment was echoed, to varying degrees, by the others.

Clearly, however, some important lessons had been learned about reform. A classroom of six teachers was too unwieldy to accommodate the rigid schedule. Interpersonal issues had to be worked out in advance. More planning time was vitally important. The teachers set down on paper a series of goals for improving the current program.

1. Must have planning period in common.
2. Reduce the number of teachers.
3. Reduce the goals for interdisciplinary functions (i.e., two subjects instead of four?).
4. Screen students better (i.e., no chronic discipline problems).
5. Improve communication with the rest of the faculty and try to do outreach to spread the principles of the program.

With mixed feelings of relief and regret, Brenda, Sam, and Clark gave over the Quest program to Ellie, Bill, and Sue. The three, it was decided, were the most compatible and had the least to lose in remaining with the program. Brenda feared she would never again teach her advanced placement class in biology if she abandoned it a second time. Clark decided that an interdisciplinary course more oriented toward math would better suit his interests. Ellie, Bill, and Sue were delighted with the prospect of working together. "I have high hopes," said Ellie, "and millions of ideas." "If not for Quest," said Bill, "I really think I would have left teaching. Hard as it is, it's the part of my day that sustains me."

5

Establishing Equilibrium
Year 2

By the fall of 1992, many of the most highly publicized school-reform efforts had begun to unravel. In Rochester, New York, the much touted experiment in teacher empowerment and restructuring was foundering on personality conflicts and fiscal woes. In Chelsea, Massachusetts, the audacious experiment of Boston University's John Silber to take over a public school system had failed miserably—again, due to interpersonal and fiscal issues. Chicago's parent boards were encountering similar difficulties. The Coalition of Essential Schools (the direct inspiration for Quest's design) issued the first of a series of ethnographic studies documenting the virtual impossibility of implementing Sizer's original program and calling for more modest change in light of the newly understood complexity of the reform process.

Sue, Bill, and Ellie opened the second year of Quest with new confidence and new direction. They had spent several weeks during the summer rethinking curriculum and reviewing the complaints and suggestions made by parents of the previous Quest class. Content was clearly an issue, as were more rigorous standards. Parents had complained that the Quest students had not done enough reading, had not been assigned sufficient vocabulary, and had written too few analytical papers. Students and parents had questioned the nature of the history curriculum embedded in Quest, asking why there was no recognizable history included and why the emphasis was so completely on creative writing.

At the same time that they were considering these various criticisms, Bill, Sue, and Ellie were becoming increasingly enmeshed in the language of the Coalition of Essential Schools. In the spring of the previous year, Brookville had agreed to become an *Exploring School,* a term used by Sizer and his organization for institutions involved in the first stages of Coalition restructuring. As an Exploring School, Brookville was granted a $5,000 stipend to be used for disseminating to the larger faculty the principles of restructuring and for visiting other institutions in more advanced stages of change. A Coalition of Essential Schools subcommittee had been estab-lished by the principal as one of a number of faculty led *goal committees.* The group was charged with considering the principles of the Coalition, with looking at Quest as an archetype for school-wide change, and with gathering information about strategies for expanding the Coalition agenda in the school. Bill, Sue, and Ellie were necessarily involved in all these activities, and they came to school in the fall speaking comfortably about *students-as-workers* and *developing habits of mind,* two of Sizer's key phrases. "This year," said Bill, when asked of his goals for the new Quest, "these kids are going to be able to think, to be able to examine problems with an open mind, to look at school as something that is challenging, not just rote memory, mechanical kinds of things. We want to develop habits of mind as a continuous activity, to have kids see the complexity of problems, not just go for the simple solutions."

On the surface at least, everything seemed infinitely easier. The schedules had emerged as promised for the three teachers, including planning periods in common and no requirements for study hall duty. The teacher team, stripped of all superfluous or prickly personalities, seemed perfectly in tune with one another. Bill and Ellie had designated themselves the English and history teachers respectively, with Sue as the roving jack-of-all-trades. "The setup seems to make sense," said Ellie, "given the more academic focus of the new course."

The theme for this year's Quest was "the city," a more manageable and concrete topic than the abstract one of "change." After a brief meeting in the fall at Blair, it was decided that the topic would be approached by focusing on the various institutions sustaining city life (e.g., schools, health care, law, and recreational facilities). As before, the topics would be introduced by visiting speakers who would be experts in each area. They would lay the informational groundwork for various projects assigned in each unit. The students would again work in groups, designing their projects as pieces of a final exhibition, to be entitled Brookville, 2030. "By grounding them in the real world," said Ellie, "we hope the work will become more rigorous. They'll have to be able to defend with facts any choice they make for their future city."

Quest started the year with a mapping unit on current Brookville, and then a unit on education and schooling. In order to answer last year's parental complaints, Bill and Ellie began the education unit with a historical look at the city's schools. A professor from Blair came to class and lectured on colonial and 19th century schooling. A yearbook project was assigned, in which students were asked to develop a profile of their own high school from the yearbook of a previous decade. Other assignments followed quickly on the heels of this one, for example, an essay on a recent school controversy and an oral report.

Students were asked to work on these various assignments in their groups and at their own pace. Meanwhile, Ellie had set about developing a new unit on law, which was rich with oral and written assignments, as well as short- and long-term projects (see Resource C). The students were to be asked to produce a large research paper, a position paper, an exhibition, a study of the school's code of conduct, and other work, all considering a wide range of legal issues from local to international.

The pace of assignments and the various rates at which students were accomplishing them began to grow dizzying. Within their groups, students displayed the same range of commitment they had shown the previous year: some deeply engaged, others distracted, and others confused. Some earlier assignments were abandoned in an effort to clear the decks. Others, completed, were never discussed.

Clearly, the rapid pace of the work stood in dramatic contrast to the meandering quality of assignments the previous year. But students seemed no less certain about where the work was going, and why it was being assigned. In October, a researcher asked students to explain some of the basic principles of Quest, and to articulate the goals behind some of their assignments.

Researcher: How is Quest different from your other classes?

Justin: Here we read novels. All the stuff we read last year was boring.

Alex: We do things with our hands; like little projects.

Amy: Because it's two periods together. We do a lot of creative work, less compositions and factual stuff.

Researcher: What do you think your teachers want you to get out of this class?

Justin: Knowledge of what's going on in the world. Being able to do things. And to read books.

Alex: A scholarly attitude, although I don't know what that means.

Amy: I think they want us to expand our vocabulary. I think they want us to be more aware of our community, because we do a lot of stuff with civics. And I think they want us to speak well in front of people because we do a lot of oral reports.

Researcher: Why do you think you have three teachers instead of one?

Justin: I really don't know. We have two because it's two periods, and like two classes. I don't know what the third is for.

Alex: With so many kids, you get more attention.

Amy: It's a really big class and it takes a long time. Mr. O. is for English. Mrs. K. is for civics. Mrs. W. is for English too. That's all I can figure.

Researcher: What do you think is the main point or goal of Quest?

Justin: I don't know. I really don't know.

Alex: To help us learn better. If you learn in a different way, to help you learn in that way.

Amy: I think it's based on social skills. In our English and our civics, we do a lot of social work. We have to develop people skills because we speak in front of people all the time.

The students understood that Quest was a class which afforded more freedom and creativity, but the larger themes and intentions of the course remained vague. In particular, the students seemed to have wholly over-looked the integrated aspect of the curriculum. They saw Quest as two separate subjects, taught by two separate teachers. Often, the first period of Quest would be devoted to English, the second period to civics. Bill (the designated English teacher) would lead the first class in a discussion of *To Kill a Mockingbird,* and then Ellie (the designated civics teacher) would have the students resume their work on the law unit. Few students, it seemed, made connections between the two periods, although connections existed in the teachers' minds.

Bill and Ellie's subject-specific roles in the Quest classroom left Sue somewhat out in the cold. Gradually, she became critical of the growing bifurcation between disciplines and what she perceived as a growing conservatism of method (i.e., the use of multiple-choice tests and textbook worksheets). As a reading teacher with years of experience in remedial instruction, she saw this conventional methodology confounding the weakest members of the class. "That child is dyslexic and you simply can't ask that of him!" she would explode occasionally at a curriculum meeting. But, most often, she said nothing. Her role, she noted, receded with every passing month.

Meanwhile, the relationship between Bill and Ellie grew deeper and deeper. Observing them on a midwinter day, a visitor would be struck by the perfect, interpersonal choreography between them: the Nick-and-Nora banter, the effortless balance of power. As one taught, the other automatically took over the menial work of classroom management, throwing jokes and remarks over his or her shoulder. The immense goodwill that seemed to characterize these interactions spread easily to the students, and they took far less time to bond than they had in the previous, chaotic year.

Reform Begins to Spread

With a formal Coalition group working in the school, talk of reform began to spread. Growing numbers of curious faculty began visiting a series of nearby Coalition schools, returning with stories of unique programs and stimulating partnerships. "I recognize that we're being shown only the very best that exists when we visit these schools," said Brenda, "but it's still impressive and inspiring."

In January, Robert McCarthy, a representative from Coalition Headquarters in Providence visited the school, observing in the Quest classroom and speaking to the assembled faculty as a whole. McCarthy, a former principal at Brookline High School, and an astute, charismatic leader, made a deep and immediate impression on the faculty. A keen, sensitive listener, practiced in the politics of change, McCarthy praised the teachers for their dedication and assured them that the difficulties they faced on a daily basis were not unique to Brookville. Sensing the paranoia about ability grouping, McCarthy assured the teachers that grouping was a nonissue and a distraction from the real problems needing to be addressed. He did not address what would become of ability grouping, but the power of his reform message seemed to dilute the tension surrounding that issue. Sympathetic, optimistic, and ecumenical, McCarthy's presentation to the faculty sparked a wave of interest and enthusiasm from a wide range of teachers who had hitherto been frightened away from reform by sticky problems of grouping. Others bristled at McCarthy's evasiveness, or simply failed to "get it."

"Maybe there's something wrong with me," said a middle-aged teacher new to the school, "but I still don't understand how this whole thing fits together. I've read the principles, I've listened to the speakers, but I can't seem to see the whole picture."

*   *   *

"Why don't you invite the faculty into Quest?" The question was asked frequently by Blair faculty and administrators. To an outsider, the reticence of Quest teachers to open their doors to their colleagues was confounding, particularly because it seemed to be the most efficient way to get teachers speaking about change in concrete terms. No longer embarrassed by the work they were doing, Bill and Ellie's antisocial nature seemed to stem more from their sense of domestic privacy. Although they professed to feel comfortable with any and all observers, the Quest classroom in fact had become an increasingly closed world, a world whose specialness derived from its intimacy.

*   *   *

In February, eight teachers, including the three Quest teachers, were granted a release day to begin exploring possibilities for the following year. Together, they drew up seven recommendations for change.

Introduction

Working with the written and verbal input of the faculty, the release group engaged in a day of dialogue considering all of the areas of interest presented to it. Based on its daylong exchange, the group has come up with the following recommendations for continued exploration and expansion of curriculum. It is the belief of the group that change takes time and that it is important that change occurs in smaller, rather than larger, increments. Some of the specific areas of interest from some of the faculty may require more time to study in terms of direct impact on the curriculum as it now stands and the day as it is now structured. However, the group did end its day with some specific recommendations, and the group believes that the level of interest exhibited by the faculty would enable the school to carry them out.

The Coalition for Essential Schools Exploration

Growing out of a discussion group with the assistance of Blair College came an interest in exploring the Coalition of Essential Schools. A Coalition group continues to exist and this year is operating with a $5000 grant to continue further exploration. This exploration has included regular meetings of the group, networking with Coalition schools and other Exploring schools, doing additional reading, inviting speakers associated with the Coalition to the school, and visiting other schools to observe firsthand some of the programs the schools have enacted.

Recommendation 1: That the Coalition group continue its exploration but in so doing develop a better means to communicate their work to the entire faculty and a means to better educate the faculty about the Quest program. While we have used grant monies to travel to other schools, we have not had our own teachers observe the program in our own school.

Recommendation 2: That the ninth grade Quest be continued and expanded to target 80 ninth-grade students. Requirements include

1. Two double-period blocks of 40 students, with two teachers assigned to each block (total = 4 teachers)
2. That the four teachers share a common planning period

Recommendation 3: That a grade 10 Quest offering be added to the curriculum with a target population of 40 students. Requirements should be the same as in #2.

Recommendation 4: That the teachers involved in all Quest blocks be afforded time to complete summer curriculum work structured in a way that is most beneficial to their efforts, and that they be allotted some release days next year as needed to fine-tune their work.

Recommendation 5: That interested teachers be encouraged and supported in developing an interdisciplinary course to begin in September of 1993 (or 1994).

Recommendation 6: That interested teachers be encouraged to use a model that has a double-period block of time. These teachers should identify their target group, determine the distribution of course credits, and request a common period for the planning essential to their efforts.

Recommendation 7: That teachers involved in such planning be given the necessary summer curriculum work days needed to develop their course and any release days needed during the year.

The recommendations received a fairly favorable response from the faculty, largely because they were presented by Jan Freeman, the 35-year veteran teacher and union representative who had lately developed an increasing interest in reform. Jan, formerly among the most skeptical and conservative of the faculty, had long had the reputation of a no-nonsense straight shooter, who moved easily between warring constituencies. No one expected Jan to join the ranks of the romantic reformers. Yet, her growing interest in Quest was a public fact. Indeed, she had managed to convince the principal to let her use her duty period to help Bill, Sue, and Ellie improve the history component of the Quest curriculum. Since September, Jan had been a fixture in the Quest classroom and a powerful public relations tool for the program. Even the most cynical naysayers could not afford to ignore a program supported by so powerful a faculty leader.

But for every step forward, there was a step back. Any growing interest in change seemed habitually thwarted by the hardships of daily life in the school. The superintendent had left the area in September for a higher paying position in Greenwich, Connecticut, dismayed by the lack of funding and by a rancorous school committee, which she claimed permitted her no leeway. No one could blame her. Articles on the high school appeared almost weekly, citing asbestos violations, ventilation problems, vandalism. There were informal conversations about becoming a Coalition school (i.e., committing to a reform effort that would be schoolwide and include dramatic changes in scheduling and curriculum). These met with little support. Invariably, such talk turned to more immediate problems. "I just don't see it happening here," said one teacher, in a roundtable discussion. "You can't ask people to give what they don't have. Most of the teachers in this school just don't have the interest or energy to completely remake their curriculum. The ones that do—let them do it. But don't force it on everybody."

A full-faculty vote in late winter confirmed the predictable. Only 15 faculty out of the entire group assembled wanted to formally affiliate with

Sizer's organization, even if their "no" vote meant they would be excluded from further Coalition funding. The principal claimed to be highly disappointed in the outcome of the poll. To the Quest faculty, the outcome was no surprise. "People in this school are just tolerant enough to allow some crazy teachers to teach their little experimental course," one teacher explained, "so long as it doesn't rock the boat too much. But that's as far as it goes. This is not a faculty that will ever buy 100% into some new program or philosophy. We're much too independent and idiosyncratic."

The faculty did vote, however, to support the expansion of Quest into three new classes—two ninth-grade sections, and a tenth-grade one. Jan Freeman and Lilly Swanson, another much-respected and veteran history teacher, signed on for the experimental program.

In Quest, students continued to move through a succession of activities and visiting speakers. In order to make each student accountable for his work, Bill, Sue, and Ellie issued Individual Checklist Forms, enumerating the many assignments required and specifying whether the rough draft, revised draft, final draft, and exhibition-perfect version of those assignments had been completed. The method helped the teachers keep track of student progress but seemed to have less effect on students themselves. Languishers still languished; workers still worked.

In interviews, the students seemed deeply split between those who loved and those who loathed the class. Enthusiasts praised the group work, its social aspects and informality. Supporters also raved about the teachers, the sense of respect they felt emanating from adults, the creative assignments, and the outside visitors. Those who liked Quest ran the gamut from academically weak to strong. The same was true of Quest's detractors. Among this group, many spoke of the wasted time, the noise and confusion, and the lack of basic skills and traditional material—all of which seemed to cause palpable anxiety in these students. "Too many people are in this program who don't want to be here. They fool around and waste time. The teachers don't seem to care. I need a quiet place to work." Then, from another student, "This is the first class I can actually work in. I need to do things my own way. The teachers respect that."

The Final Exhibition, Year 2

That great discrepancy in response showed itself on the night of the final exhibition. Again, dressed with uncharacteristic polish, the 40 Quest students waited nervously with their displays in the health room as parents and other visitors were briefed by Bill in the school's theater. The crowd was extremely thin, a fact that seemed to surprise visitors as they entered the room. A local dance recital was being held in another part of the school, and the parking lot was filled to overflowing with cars.

Inside, tawdry music drifted into the theater, and little girls in tutus peeked in as Bill spoke to the assembled group, "This is the second year of Quest's public exhibition," he began. "This year, in response to parent input in the past, there has been a greater focus on writing. Visitors should be able to see this in the materials displayed."

A nearby parent leaned in to another one. "My son can't write a single grammatical sentence," she whispered.

"This exhibition is the culmination of the students' yearlong thinking and working on the subject of the city. But it is only in the last two or three weeks that the students have taken their work seriously. Although we have told them many times, 'the public is coming,' they only responded at the very end."

Many parents shuffled in their seats at this, an odd disclaimer to preface a presentation.

Bill distributed a Final Exhibition Evaluation Sheet and a list of criteria for parents to use in assessing what they saw (see Resource D). The forms required parents to evaluate the work of each group as a whole, and also of individual presenters. "Each student is accountable to his team and also responsible for himself," Bill said. "Please respond with kindness, but also with candor. The kids really appreciate your comments."

"I want to say," continued Bill, his voice softer, "that preparing for this exhibition has been very hectic for all of us. As teachers, we are pulled in every direction. Teacher burnout is always looming around every corner. There are kids breathing down your neck continuously. But, it's a process that really gets you close to the kids in a positive way. A deep fondness develops, a relationship you can't get in other classes. And when we ask ourselves, 'Are these kids getting something out of public education?'— even on the hardest days, the answer is a resounding 'Yes!' "

In the exhibition room itself, students stood before their scant displays with the same confidence and poise their counterparts had shown the year before. A similar blend of knowledge, ignorance, and arrogance characterized their responses. One group had renamed Brookville "Dumpville" because "the town will be destroyed in 2000, and rebuilt with junk from local dumps." Another group proposed that a football stadium be built in Brookville with capital raised from a gambling casino. One group proposed meeting the needs of the elderly by "putting a phone in every room so they can call to go to the hospital."

Amidst the pockets of shoddy work were examples of the exceptional. A dark-haired boy, Nick, displayed a series of beautifully rendered graphs depicting various aspects of the police department and tracing changes in rates and types of crimes in the city. Explaining his work in a clear, strong voice, he listened intently as a math teacher suggested several improvements in the display of his statistics.

The following afternoon, the teachers sat together reviewing the evaluation sheets collected the night before. Some offered troubling comments: "Blatantly rude!" "Didn't know his stuff at all." Most, however, were complimentary to the point of excess:"Brilliant work!" "I'm profoundly impressed!"

"Look at the spelling and grammar on these things," laughed Ellie. "The kids filled these out themselves!"

"Well, I guess if we accomplished nothing else," laughed Sue, "we sure did instill in them high self-esteem!"

6

Settling In
Year 3

A New Beginning

No one had believed that Quest would survive beyond its initial turbulent year. As late as April and May of that first year, teachers had talked openly and with derision about the failed experiment in Room 201. Midyear, even the Quest teachers had talked of the program in retrospective terms: "It could have been a good program," they had said, "if only times were different, budgets were different, leadership was different."

But Quest did survive, and by the end of its second full year of implementation, few questioned its inevitable place in the school culture. By late spring of the previous year, some subtle change of attitude had worked its way into the consciousness of Brookville High School. Now, in the fall of the third year, there seemed to be a marked shift, a new acceptance of the inevitability of change among the great majority of teachers, old and new, conservative and liberal.

How the high school moved from pervasive cynicism to frail belief cannot be wholly attributed to any one event or individual. Nor can the change in attitude be described in especially positive terms. It seems, instead, to have emerged partly as a result of the faculty's continuous proximity to reform dogma; a kind of conversion through immersion. The steady stream of visiting Coalition speakers, the endless and confused talk of restructuring, the reports from philosophy committees, faculty Coalition task forces, and teacher focus groups all served to make change a familiar, even homey, term. Those who once saw the language of Coalition reform as threatening had been quietly and inexorably lulled by its mantra.

Also influential in moving the faculty toward acceptance was the change in the principal's attitude toward reform. Once defensive from the school's bad press and from other outside criticism, Fitzgerald had come to embrace Coalition doctrine with a fierce enthusiasm. Indeed, his early reticence toward change had been replaced by passionate support. He accompanied the Quest teachers on trips to other schools; he expressed unconditional support for those who wished to experiment with new formats in their classes (still bound, of course, by the constraints of the schedule and the budget); and he agitated the faculty to vote themselves formally affiliated with the Coalition. Fitzgerald's interest in the Coalition seemed to catch the faculty off guard. Although some took his support as a reason in itself to reject change, others felt his newfound support would ease the transition toward reform. For most, Fitzgerald's enthusiasm merely seemed to reinforce the fact that change was inevitable.

There was, however, one outside factor that ultimately forced even the most stalwart cynics to cease criticism of the reform agenda. In the spring of Quest's second year, the Massachusetts legislature passed a massive educational-reform bill mandating an array of changes in school policy and curriculum. For teachers, the bill had an especially fearsome clause: It eliminated all tenure and rendered invalid teachers' permanent certifications. Even longtime veterans of the classroom would now be obliged to re-earn their teaching certificates on an ongoing basis. Many of the teachers at Brookville High School interpreted the new law as a threat to their jobs. Teachers who would not comply with policy changes or who resisted mandates for reform could conceivably have their contracts terminated. Although, in truth, such action was highly implausible (contracts still had tough "just cause" clauses), the bill had sufficient bite to snuff out all vocal resistance to reform policies.

So it was that, with the opening of school in Quest's third year, the faculty seemed to have assumed a tame, compliant quality dramatically different from its affect 2 years before. Teachers no longer spoke in dismissive tones of the Quest Program, now expanded by the earlier faculty vote to include two sections of freshmen (Quest I and Quest II), and one of sophomores (Sophomore Quest I). This made the reform presence in the school a considerable one. Students involved in Quest programs now numbered more than 100, and six teachers now devoted some part of their days to the program.

* * *

Now, on the first day of school in Bill and Ellie's classroom, Quest seemed to have been transformed into a perfectly choreographed pas de deux. The chaos and contradiction of previous beginnings was replaced by a kind of fetish for organization, which showed itself in every aspect of the curriculum. Students, subdued by nervousness and the heat of the day, filed in quietly to a class carefully decorated with posters and large, neatly written signs. "Today's Agenda," had been written by Ellie on top of the board, and then next to it: "Skills of Good Listeners: Focusing, Note-Taking, Questioning." The morning's work would be composed of roll call, a stern enumeration of the rules of the classroom, and then an introduction to the first English assignment, *Lord of the Flies*. Ellie had xeroxed pages from a model log that demonstrated ways students might respond in writing to their reading assignments each week. The log was a requirement of the class. "There are three acceptable uses of the log," Ellie read aloud from her handout. "Questioning, reacting, and criticizing." She went on to discuss each approach at length, while students sat with stony faces or wrote notes in the margins of their sheets.

The theme of the third year's Quest was "Justice in America," but students would not be introduced to that theme, or indeed to any of the Coalition goals or principles, until later in the month. "Ellie and I are taking a more incremental approach this year," Bill explained, during a break in the morning. "We're trying to inch our way in to the innovative stuff." Two years of experience proved that to move directly into the thematic work was agitating and confusing to the ninth graders. Instead, the teachers of Quest I would slip quietly into the project format. This time, they would ease the class gradually into group work, making sure that the students first understood the idea of individual accountability.

"Last year," laughed Ellie, "we really freaked them out. But, we didn't have our own act together as much then."

"In any case, we want to make sure we're developing some measurable skills and covering content. That's what everyone complained about last year, not enough content."

One clear sign of the concern for content could be seen in the structure of Quest itself. The shift away from a truly interdisciplinary format (which began the year before) seemed to have become solidified into policy now. Although classroom management was neatly shared by the two teachers, the content was clearly delineated. Bill was the English teacher; Ellie was the civics teacher. Most frequently, each of the two periods was devoted to a different discipline. While Bill opened his discussion of *Lord of the Flies,* warning students to be alert for symbolism and images "that are going to come back later in the book," Ellie distributed worksheets, modeled on the board on how to take notes, and shuffled attendance cards. Later, as Ellie introduced the civics book, Bill would perform similar duties. "This format," said Ellie, "is much easier to control." And, indeed, the students seemed content with the traditional format. There was none of the visceral agitation that invariably struck the visitors to last year's Quest class.

Although the move toward a more traditional format may have offered the teachers new grounding, real control still remained elusive. Again, in this third year, despite everyone's best intentions, terrible and unexpected problems had complicated Quest's life.

The first of those problems came from the union. Two weeks after the end of last year, the union called a *work-to-rule* slowdown over a contract dispute. Under work-to-rule, union members were not to do any extra work outside of their basic teaching responsibilities. Work-to-rule persisted all summer long, confounding the plans of teachers who had intended to do curriculum work for Quest. Bill, Ellie, Sue, and Jan (the teachers of Quests I and II) had expected to spend much of the summer developing elaborate curriculum plans for their courses. The work-to-rule slowdown made them feel too guilty to meet on a regular basis, and they consequently had done only the bare minimum of preparation before school started. Several of the Quest teachers had also enrolled in a special Coalition summer workshop in New Hampshire, a 1-week course promising to illustrate how to disseminate Sizer's principles to a reluctant faculty. Participation in that had also been canceled.

Other problems followed. Two days before school began, Jan (the new "history half" of Quest II) was notified that she had been granted early retirement, to commence at once. Although Jan had put in for the retirement package the previous spring, the state's silence had led her to believe that she had been passed over. Now, with no formal curriculum in place and the prospect of a brand new teacher in the team, Quest II's English teacher was in an understandable panic. Although Jan volunteered to stay on at no pay until a suitable replacement was found, her loss was a serious blow to the program. As the president of the union and a longtime faculty advocate,

Jan's active support for Quest had done wonders for the program's public relations.

Perhaps the biggest work-to-rule casualty of all was the new sophomore section of Quest, run by Sue and a history teacher new to the Quest format. These teachers had also accepted the union's mandate and had refused to meet during the summer months. They now began the year almost blindly, without either a fleshed out curriculum or a precedent to serve as a guide. "We'll just have to wing it," said the history teacher. "I have a good sense of humor. I expect it will carry me at least to October."

In terms of scheduling, however, the Quest program had made progress. The seventh period every day was the Quest conference period: Finally, after 2 years of unsuccessful efforts, the Quest teachers had a free period in common. The period was devoted to talking shop, laying out the week's curriculum, coordinating assignments in the two classes, and sharing insights about students.

On this afternoon in September, Ellie opened the meeting by talking about numbers. There were 73 students in the two sections of freshman Quest, and the rooms were jam-packed. After some negotiating with the principal during lunch, Bill reported that he been promised a third room. Sue reminded the group that originally 84 students had been signed up for the class. She and Ellie had to speak personally with the middle school guidance department in order to get ten of them reassigned to more appropriate placements in the high school resource room. "They're still trying to use us as a special ed dumping ground. We're not a special ed class. But they can't seem to understand that."

Sue reported on the progress of the day in Quest II. Rather than begin with *Lord of the Flies*, she and Jan had decided to start with several chapters from *Horace's Compromise* (Sizer's book on school reform). Less leery than Bill and Ellie about introducing the Coalition agenda, Sue hoped to use the Sizer chapters as a lead-in to "what Quest is all about."

"Tell us how it goes," said Ellie.

"Once we outline the common principles of Quest," continued Sue, "we hope to get into the civics—civic virtues and dispositions."

"Do you see this leading to a large expository essay?" Bill asked.

"We were thinking more in terms of eulogies. We were hoping that if the kids wrote eulogies for themselves it would provide grist for a good discussion of personal virtues. And from there, we'd move to civic virtues."

Bill and Ellie wrote this down. "This is good. This is useful *and* good."

Indeed, the talk throughout the meeting was focused and constructive. The four teachers, clearly good friends, exchanged useful tips, self-deprecating jokes, and ideas for assignments. There was little discussion of student behavior, and, so far, no scheduling or budgetary problems to contend with. At the same time, there was little idealism. Time after time, interesting, innovative ideas would be shot down with a perfunctory quip: "Too expensive." "Can't fit it into the schedule." "No support." Such quips were met with wry laughter.

"Well," sighed Jan, "We'll do the best we can." It was almost 5:00 p.m., and the teachers had all been at the school since 7:00 a.m. The silence of the empty school had filtered into our classroom, and the little band of reformers began to pack up their books.

"This *all* feels good," said Ellie. "Do you think maybe we're actually on track this year?" She looked at Bill and Sue and Jan with raised eyebrows and a coy smirk. Two years of struggle passed before our collective imagination.

"Too early to say," said Jan, and everyone nodded.

*   *   *

Brookville High School
Quest Program, 1993-1994

The Quest Program has been designed around a set of common principles drawn from the common principles of the Coalition of Essential Schools. Established in 1984 as a high school/university partnership, the Coalition is based at Brown University and chaired by Theodore Sizer. Although not yet a Coalition school, Brookville High School has been an "Exploring school" for the past 2 years. As such, we have discussed and debated these common principles and have visited Coalition schools throughout New England to view these ideas in action.

Using these principles as our guide, the Quest Program sets its goals and learning outcomes around a pre-established list of essential skills and a selected body of knowledge. The intent is to produce a student who will be able to demonstrate a mastery of these skills and knowledge emanating from the selected curriculum.

THE COMMON PRINCIPLES OF THE QUEST PROGRAM

1. The program will focus on students learning to use their minds well.

2. The goals will be simple: Each student will master a limited number of essential skills and areas of knowledge.

3. "Less is more" will dominate curriculum decisions, which will be guided by an aim at student mastery and achievement, rather than an effort merely to cover content.

4. The governing principles of the program will be *student-as-worker* rather than *teacher-as-deliverer-of-instruction.* Students will learn how to learn and how to teach themselves.

5. The tone of this program will stress values of expectation, of trust (until abused), and of decency (i.e., tolerance, respect, and sensitivity).

6. At the end of the course, students will present a final exhibition to demonstrate their grasp of the central skills and knowledge of the program.

SKILLS
Students should be able to

- think critically by identifying problems, asking essential questions, analyzing material, and drawing conclusions based on substantiation of ideas based on evidence
- present ideas and information in oral, visual, and written form
- write clearly and persuasively
- carry out independent research
- conduct a personal interview
- work cooperatively and productively in groups
- assume responsibility for individual and group work
- display organizational skills
- develop a plan of action with timelines for completion
- develop positive attitudes toward work
- develop a willingness to accept responsibility for one's own decisions and the consequences of such decisions
- interact with others with tolerance, respect, and sensitivity

ESSENTIAL QUESTIONS
The Grade 9 Quest curriculum is built around the essential question "What is justice in America?" Using the skills they are

learning and practicing and the materials presented in class, the
students will build a base of knowledge to use in pursuing this
question.

KNOWLEDGE
    Students should

- acquire an understanding of those dispositions and values
  that lead to the healthy functioning of a democracy
- recognize the conflicts and dilemmas in American society
  that surround the debate over how the fundamental values
  of American democracy should be enacted
- explore the purposes of law in society and the characteristics of good laws
- understand the basic structure of American government
- recognize that constitutional democracy has been and is an
  evolutionary process
- understand the rights and responsibilities of citizens
- understand the structure and functioning of the American
  legal system

PART

2

REFORM IN PERSPECTIVE

7

Players in Reform

Teachers, Students, Administrators, and Consultants

The second half of this book is devoted to a consideration of the meaning of Quest's story and its significance in the larger picture of school change. As the introduction to the volume asserted, the unfolding trials and tribulations of the Brookville High School teachers, students, administrators, and consultants are being reenacted in high schools across America, wherever site-based reforms are underway. Despite all the regional differences that define schools and all the individual personalities that define educators and students, there is still, inevitably, much that is similar. A case study, by definition, demonstrates that similarity even as it develops for the reader a unique and idiosyncratic story.

In this chapter, I consider closely the roles of each of the various players in the story of Quest. I begin with the constituency that is clearly most central to the story: the teachers who designed and implemented the reform initiatives. The difficulty of their work is summarized first. Then, the impact of reform on teachers is explored. What is gained and lost in the process of designing, teaching, and promoting a program such as this one? The chapter considers the bottom line for teachers, both from their own and from this author's perspectives.

Next, the chapter considers the impact of a program such as Quest upon students. Any reader of the preceding story will already have recognized the ambiguous nature of success in the Quest classroom. Like every other aspect of this story, the students' gains and losses are subjective and relative to the goals of those doing the measuring. Reported here are the results of surveys of Quest students and follow-up interviews with Quest "graduates." These data document the students' perceptions of the program.

Following this, the roles of the principal and superintendent in the reform process are discussed. It is easy to blame these administrators for the problems and confusions plaguing the first year of Quest's implementation. However, the chapter argues that the administrators were themselves locked into untenable roles, which made meaningful support of reform virtually impossible.

Finally, the chapter looks closely at the role of the consultant, considering both the inside consultants from Blair College and the outside consultants from the Coalition. How did the teachers' perceptions of college faculty shift with the changing fortunes of reform efforts? How intimately should the fate of the college be tied to the fate of a program it supported and nurtured? I have tried to answer these questions, both in the context of the Blair/Brookville collaboration, and in a larger context as well.

The Teachers

So much has been written on the plight of the American teacher, both historically and today, that a recitation of the woes of the teacher reads like a cliché. Willard Waller's (1932) *Sociology of Teaching* first formally articulated what teachers and their families had known for generations: that classroom teachers were overworked and undervalued; that the two-tier system of school governance (which separated and elevated administrators) infantilized teachers; and that communities set up unrealistic expectations for teachers, judging their teachers as they would no other civil servant. Dan Lortie's (1975) sociology of the teaching profession demonstrated how little things had changed for teachers in a century marked by so many other kinds of liberation. The teachers in Lortie's study were still isolated, conservative, and fearful. The ground that might have been gained in the 1960s through the institution of collective bargaining was lost in public backlash and suspicion. Even with a union to back them, high school teachers continued to work under difficult conditions, teaching an average of 140 students a day. Despite progress made in salaries, most teachers in America still earn less than skilled laborers (Warren, 1990).

Contemporary teacher autobiographies, which depict firsthand the daily realities of the teacher's job, illustrate why the profession is so quickly abandoned by its most gifted new recruits. The following excerpt from Stuart Palonsky's (1986) book, *900 Shows a Year,* vividly describes the unnerving sequence of a new teacher's work day:

> The school day sped by quickly. There was little time to think about what you were doing or reflect on the consequences of your actions. From the first bell to the last, we were always rushing. There was always work to do, papers to grade, tests to run off and material to duplicate. When I first started teaching in the school, I noticed that most of my colleagues were always busy with papers and grade books. By the second week I no longer noticed because I was consumed with my own work, most of it clerical. I had to check attendance lists, prepare homework assignments for absent students, keep track of tests and makeup exams, and maintain a record of those students who were failing and those who were not working hard. . . . At times I thought I did more grading and testing than teaching.
>
> For the most part, one day blended in with the next, with little to distinguish one from another. I saw the same students at the same time every day. I passed the same teachers and students in the hall at the same place and time every day. I said hello to the same people as often as a dozen times a day, but I rarely engaged any of them in more substantive conversation. . . .
>
> I found it difficult to teach well. Preparing for class, devising strategies, finding materials, and presenting them to students took more time and energy than I had. It was hard enough to teach thirty students well any one period, and perhaps too unrealistic to expect to do it five times a day. . . . If I really tried hard, I could teach three to four good classes a day, and I could usually do this about two or three times a week. I told one of the teachers of my frustration. He told me that if I were a baseball player and went two for five everyday, I would be a .400 hitter. No one has hit like that since Ted Williams, he said by way of consolation. Who did I think I was, anyway? (pp. 81-82)

The kinds of demands and expectations depicted in this passage lead invariably to compromises of the sort Sizer (1984) refers to in *Horace's*

Compromise. Teachers in America typically assign less writing than they should, fail to follow up on every problem that needs resolving, and exert less energy preparing than they would like to. Working day after day at a job that requires such compromises takes an enormous psychic toll. Seeing one's best efforts consistently produce second-rate results is obviously demoralizing and depressing. Studies of teacher attrition consistently attribute burnout to just such factors.[1]

For the teachers at Brookville High School, the overwork and the repetitive aspect of their jobs were certainly factors in explaining the endemic malaise in the school. But equally critical was their sense of being undervalued and unappreciated; factors less concrete and therefore less easy to address and repair. Jan Freeman's experience in the last weeks of her 35-year career illustrate almost in caricature a problem that exists in school districts across America. A venerated school leader, teaching honors American history and the new, experimental Quest program, Jan's imminent retirement might have sparked a difficult, months-long search for a replacement. Indeed, were Jan a veteran doctor or a partner in a law firm, a search for her replacement would have been national in scope. Instead, Jan reported, the position was advertised in the last week of August (one week before school was to start). The job was listed only in the local want ads under an advertisement for "Truckdrivers, part-time." "What a testament to the importance of my 35-year career," said Jan. Indeed, teachers at Brookville often noted that the real, intellectual nature of their work was wholly ignored in a system (like most systems) obsessed with organizational concerns. "Each month the school committee awards an Employee of the Month citation to a district worker," Jan says. "It almost never goes to a teacher. The last time it did, a middle school teacher was cited for 'putting up with the skunk smell outside her window.' "

Sarason (1990) sees this devaluing of the teacher's work as a conspiracy to maintain power in the hands of a ruling administration. Worthlessness and powerlessness reinforce one another, maintaining (despite talk of reform and restructuring) a stubborn status quo. Teachers are lured into reform programs with the promise of self-rule and empowerment only to find themselves doubly burdened by their traditional roles and new ones as well. Instead of changing the fundamental nature of the teacher's job, most reforms simply add on additional tasks and expectations. Brookville High School teachers took on the challenge of Quest as a sixth class, giving up little or nothing of their traditional workload to accommodate the experimental program. Under these conditions, reform and risk taking become a kind of punishment, and participating teachers are exhausted and overwhelmed by the very innovations that were supposed to renew them.

One Unquestioned Success

The fact is that most reform is done at the expense of the teacher. But, this need not be so. Modest administrative concessions can apparently make an enormous difference in a teacher's work day. Indeed, if Quest is any indication, it takes very little to revitalize and renew receptive veteran faculty. When relieved of their "duty" periods and given a realistic work assignment with shared time for planning, the four teachers who persisted with Quest ultimately fell in love with the innovative work they were doing.

The basic characteristics of the Quest Program (i.e., the team structure and interdisciplinary format) seem, by their very nature, to redress many of the most serious problems historically associated with the profession. The isolation, the uncertainty, the lack of adult feedback, and the lack of psychic rewards—traits cited by Lortie (1975), Goodlad (1990), and others—were all resolved to a greater or lesser degree by the Quest format and the relationships it fostered.

Gains achieved by the Quest teachers seem to fall into two categories: psychic and professional. Psychic gains refer to changes in the teachers' self-esteem and enthusiasm for their work. Typically, Bill, Ellie, and Sue speak about the "renewed energy" and "revitalizing force" derived from teaming. "Having two or three teachers together," says Sue, "gives you the feeling that you can handle anything. You can do anything. It's a great feeling of power. There's always backup, always support." "This has been a really wonderful thing for me," says Ellie. "[Teaming has] revitalized my interest in teaching. I look at what I do when I'm teaching now and really enjoy it. I don't think that many of the other teachers in the school could say that." Sue adds, "Unless you're teaching with other teachers, you really can't understand the kind of high you can get. It's exhilarating. Honestly exhilarating. Having someone there to react to you, to pat you on the back, to give you honest feedback. It's an incredible feeling."

Bill, Ellie, and Sue speak passionately too about the professional growth Quest has fostered. Ellie tells how the power to make decisions in Quest has inspired her. "Since my involvement in Quest, I find I'm doing more professional reading. I'm asking more questions, taking more responsibility. I think it's the freedom to make decisions in the class that has spurred me on; being on the firing line all the time, without anyone to guide us. Once you start going with that kind of power, it's hard to stop."

All three teachers also claim that the lessons of pedagogy worked out in Quest have been carried into their other classes. Bill claims, for example, to have learned from Quest the benefits of student rewriting. In all his classes now, students are allowed to rewrite their papers for a higher grade. All are more sensitive to individual differences in learners, and to the range of intelligence that students bring to a classroom. Cooperative learning and group projects, refined in the crucible of the Quest classroom, are now standard practice in all these teachers' classes. Ellie says she has come to rethink all the materials she uses. Now a Spanish teacher outside of Quest, she routinely uses resources from other disciplines in her Spanish classes.

Studies of school change rarely focus on this spillover effect of innovation into traditional classes. Such changes are subtle and hard to measure, but I suspect that many of them last longer than the innovative programs themselves. Long after Madeline Hunter's (1991) techniques were rejected by a district, useful threads of her program no doubt persisted in isolated classrooms.

Clearly, the interpersonal aspect of the work is the overriding reward of Quest. Studies of teachers working together invariably corroborate this fact.[2] But collegiality of the sort described by the Quest teachers is not an automatic by-product of teaming. Hargreaves and Dawes (1989) have distinguished between *contrived collegiality* (characterized by formal, bureaucratic relationships, as in assigned mentoring programs) and a true *collaborative culture* (which is organic and often slow in the making). Indeed, those very interpersonal aspects of Quest that would ultimately be perceived as its greatest reward were seen early on by the feuding teachers as its greatest liability. In early interviews during the first year of implementation, many of the six teachers called the combative adult relationships in Quest the most difficult aspect of their generally difficult work. Clark summed up the feelings of all the teachers by saying, "It's been deeply disappointing to me how we can't get along."

When the team was composed of an arbitrarily assembled group of teachers, few benefits could be derived from their relationships. It was only when teachers consciously chose their partners, thereby purposely controlling the adult relationships in the class, that rewards were felt. Philosophical and ideological differences, which might make for pleasant dinner-party debate, create chaotic tension in teamed classrooms. Personalities and temperaments must mesh from the start: Simple proximity and shared goals cannot be counted on to make for a peaceful partnership.

Insiders Versus Outsiders

To date, the greatest liability for the Quest teachers has been in another area of interpersonal relations: those between the Quest group and the other teachers in the school. As evidenced throughout the narrative, teachers were continuously at odds with the larger community in the building, and they suffered from their status as "insiders." Much has been written in reform literature about this phenomenon of separation, which seems to almost endemic in school change efforts.[3] Sizer (1992) and many of his Coalition researchers in their own work have written extensively about this tendency to isolate and even revile those involved in reform efforts. Indeed, based on these understandings, Sizer advocates a *whole school* policy on change: either everyone buys in, or the change must be rejected. Small pockets of reform create a toxic political climate that is ultimately self-defeating.

Persuasive as Sizer's reasoning is, Brookville, like many other Coalition "Exploring" schools, knew that a consensus vote for change would have great difficulty passing. Like many high schools, Brookville has a faculty profoundly divided in its values, beliefs, and talents. Three years of in-depth discussions on philosophies and goals had brought the staff no closer to a vote on joining the Coalition. Lacking a consensus, but not content to reject the possibility of change, the Quest teachers moved forward with their work in what has to be described as a generally hostile environment.

Even in the second year of implementation, long after the worst tensions had subsided, Ellie still felt acutely the sense of her own alienation. "I think [some faculty] resent us. They think we think we're on some kind of higher echelon. They resent what they see as perks: our common planning period and no study hall. There are a lot of feelings of inequity. Last year, at the final exhibition, I don't think there was one faculty member who stopped by to see what we were doing. And you get comments with an edge: 'So, what miracles did you pull off in your classroom today?' or 'Oh, I see you've come down out of your little room to be with us.' "

Tensions between outsiders and insiders predictably contributed to the deepening closeness of those involved in Quest. But such tensions also seemed to irritate the reform faculty's already problematic relationship with the administration. Quest teachers complained that the job of selling the program and winning over the other teachers to a range of reform initiatives had fallen squarely on their own overburdened shoulders. Administrators, although sympathetic and supportive in the abstract, "can never fully understand the scope, the burden." Indeed, the school administration, despite increasing efforts to accommodate the needs of the reform team, remained peripheral figures in the teachers' minds. The teachers had never fully excused the administrators for their "betrayal" in the first year of implementation (when the promises regarding the schedule and planning periods were summarily broken). They continued to see the administration as a fair-weather friend, one to be counted on when things go smoothly. "You'll see [them] until there's a problem. Then [they're] out the door."

The Students

The impact of Quest on the students in the class is less easy to determine. Certainly, it was the students who had taken the brunt of the many curricular and interpersonal mistakes characterizing the program's brief history. In the first chaotic year of Quest, ten students had dropped out of the program by mid-October. In its second year, the attrition rate was lower, but students still struggled in the early months (and some, throughout the year) to accommodate to the freedom of the group work and the rapid sequence of assignments.

Assessing the benefits and liabilities of the Quest program on students is also complicated by the class's dramatic heterogeneity. There was a great range of abilities and backgrounds among the students. As suggested in the narrative, the Quest class drew into its ranks some of the most difficult and troubled students in the middle school. In both the first and second years of implementation, guidance counselors persistently regarded the course as a progressive alternative to the beleaguered special education program. Despite efforts by the Quest faculty themselves (including direct conversations with middle school personnel), Quest invariably found within its ranks students whose emotional and intellectual deficits made independent work impossible. Although these troubled students represented only a minority of the heterogeneously grouped class, they were clearly a vocal and disruptive minority whose presence compromised the program's goals of collaboration and democratic decision making.

On the other end of the spectrum were a small minority of students capable of honors-level work and classified as gifted. Their parents had chosen Quest because of its impressive mission statements and also because of their dissatisfaction with the traditional academic program. It was to these parents that the Quest teachers felt most answerable and with whom they felt most vulnerable. As many studies of college-bound students have pointed out, grading, testing, and class rank is always an ongoing concern among this constituency.[4] Indeed, based on criticism from these students and their parents, Quest teachers turned increasingly in their second year toward the very traditional techniques and methods that the course had initially been designed to reject.

With chronic disruption on one side and demands for greater convention on another, the students in the middle could easily have been ignored. On any given day, a visitor moving from group to group might see the two dramatic ends of the spectrum (the hard worker and the disrupter) and miss the other students who were writing, lounging, or conversing quietly among themselves. It is this group that the Quest teachers knew they needed to reach, not only to prove the success of what they were doing, but also because this middle group was itself highly vulnerable to corruption. On bad days, the entire class seemed seduced into chaos by the few who were always out of control.

Self-Esteem and Social Skills

Interviews suggest that, for the students (as it had been for the teachers), the overriding success of the Quest program was in the realm of interpersonal relations.[5] By the end of both the first and second years, the students had clearly formed deep attachments to each another and to the teachers they interacted with so intimately. Students expressed frequently in interviews their sense that they were both known and "heard." Many claimed to feel powerful in class, to be conscious that their input influenced decisions about curriculum, and to believe the teachers liked them for themselves instead of for what they produced. The value of high self-esteem as an outcome of schooling is of particular importance given the population of students assigned to Quest. Many arrived at high school already cynical and defeated. As the narrative made clear, Quest accepted into its ranks students on the brink of dropping out who had never felt success in any measure in their years at school. Studies by Michael Fullan (1991; Fullan & Estabrook, 1973) and others have demonstrated both the importance and the rarity of this kind of growth in public-school settings. Fullan found that fewer than 15% of students surveyed felt their opinions and ideas were considered by their teachers. Furthermore, fewer than 25% felt their teachers heard their point of view. In Quest, not a single student in a class of 40 disagreed with the survey statement, "Teachers in Quest care about my opinion and take my point of view into consideration." Of the 40 students, 38 agreed strongly with the statement, "Quest has made me feel better about school." Certainly, even the most conservative critic of the self-esteem movement would not argue with the value of raising morale and creating positive attitudes such as these.

A follow-up study of nine randomly chosen former Quest students now in regular sophomore classes suggested that, even after a year away from the program, Quest's interpersonal benefits still resonated. Asked what the most positive aspect of Quest had been for them, seven of the nine students cited "working with others; cooperation and compromise" as the primary benefit of the class. Even when asked what they learned from the city project (a question pertaining directly to the content of the curriculum), the overwhelming majority of students still focused their responses on interpersonal issues. "How to share ideas," "how to work in groups," and "how to be tolerant of different kinds of kids" were typical answers.

Indeed, the students seemed to develop from their groups a hyperawareness of the strengths and weaknesses of their peers. Each group member could speak with certainty about the skills of other members, and these assessments would invariably be made without judgment. As illustrated several times in the narrative story of Quest, individual group members might, without self-consciousness, praise their own writing skills and then go on to cite the superior artistic or analytical skills of a peer.

Competition

Competition seemed virtually nonexistent in the evolving family of Quest. I believe this was so for a number of reasons, some positive and some negative. The warm relationships developed in group work seemed to distract students from their natural tendency to compare products. Many students genuinely saw *process* as more important than *product* and spoke with pride about their most meager efforts.

But the lack of competition may also be explained by the apparent lack of powerful incentives to perform at one's best. Intellectual excellence was valued, but it did not seem to be the first priority in the Quest class. Instead, sociability, kindness, and creativity were traits that were praised and stressed. High standards seemed difficult to maintain in a class so characterized by diversity and tolerance. Success was easy to achieve, and minimal work was rewarded greatly. The positive credo of Quest seemed to produce students with high self-esteem but with less doggedness and seriousness of purpose than a less egalitarian environment might have produced.

The lack of intellectual rigor in the first 2 years of the Quest Program was clearly its greatest liability for the students. In both the first and second years, try as they might, the teachers had difficulty drawing disciplined, critical thinking from their students and raising the academic aspects of the course above the social ones. In the follow-up interviews with Quest graduates, these students frequently mentioned the intellectual deficits that they currently felt as a result of their year in the alternative program. Asked, "In what ways are you different from other students because of your experience in Quest?" alumni most frequently responded that they now felt "academically disadvantaged" with their skills wanting in vocabulary, essay writing, and reading analysis. Asked what the most negative aspect of the class had been, the students responded candidly that the work was not rigorous enough.

In the second year, the teachers attempted to address the academic shortcomings cited by the graduates of the first year. However, follow-up interviews of these students produced similar answers. Those who disliked the program did so because they felt it academically shortchanged them. "I look back at how much time I wasted, the class wasted, in messing around and I can't believe it now. I'm getting a low B in English now, and I think it's because I didn't learn how to do serious English work in Quest. I just never worked hard there."

A second concern voiced by students in both the first and second years of Quest concerned climate. Those students who claimed to be troubled by the chaotic environment in the classroom invariably put the blame for the chaos on the teachers. They complained that the teachers didn't know "how to control kids" or "anything about discipline."

It is hard to separate the positive outcome of student empowerment from these kinds of disciplinary woes. The very traits most valued in the class—its democratic structure, its sensitivity to student input—seemed, in the Quest classroom, integrally related to the rowdiness and license that these students criticized. Both students and teachers seemed uncertain of where the balance should fall.

The Administration

A reader reaching this point in the book may well wonder about the roles of the principal and the superintendent in the story of Quest. Their presence is referred to only rarely in the narrative, and both administrators grow increasingly scarce as the story of Quest's implementation unfolds. The absence of administrators from the story of Quest is not an oversight, nor is it a unique characteristic of Quest's particular history. Indeed, narrative tales of school change, few as they are, frequently omit mention of the principal and superintendent, except as shadowy figures observing from the periphery. Even in *Horace's School,* Theodore Sizer's (1992) ideal scenario of change, the administrator is depicted as a secondary player, whose role is one of simply reacting to ideas and concerns generated by reform-minded faculty.

In one sense, the fact that reform can obviously happen without direct help from administrators is a strange and surprising discovery. Every student of school reform knows that the principal is supposed to be the pivotal figure in school change efforts. Decades of reform literature have stressed this fact, calling change virtually impossible in the absence of a powerful leader.[6] The principal, as the platitude goes, is the "gatekeeper of change"; the source of vision, the cheerleader, and the safety net for risk taking. The ideal leader would be one who could inspire faculty to make change, ameliorate difficulties when they arose, and provide the support and resources necessary to sustain the changes once they had been started.

Is such a leader realistically possible? As described here, real-life school change bears little resemblance to the easy programmatic models purveyed by professional reformers. So, too, are real-life school administrators inhibited from being the strong, consistent, and visionary reformers described in much of the popular literature on change. A close consideration of the realistic demands and pressures on both the principal and superintendent suggest how difficult it is for these administrators to spearhead or sustain risky innovation.

In the first place, the demands placed on the principal and the superintendent are in opposition to each other. The superintendent is, by nature, a political animal whose success in his job is measured by quick visible results. A superintendent must campaign on the platform of his past achievements. As a consequence, most superintendents' careers are exercises in the making of new programs and policies. Because the average tenure in office for school superintendents is brief, their focus is necessarily on the start-up, advertising, and promoting of programs, rather than on following through and perfecting the programs. Superintendents, then, want innovation to materialize quickly. They have little patience for the slow, grinding pace of institutional change. Indeed, they may well have moved on to another community by the time a new program reaches the implementation stage.

For school principals, the opposite is true. There is little incentive to move quickly or, indeed, to make any change at all. Unlike superintendents, principals must deal directly on a day-to-day basis with a range of moody constituencies—teachers, parents, and students. Principals must field complaints from these individuals without losing the goodwill necessary for the peaceful existence of their schools.

Although the superintendents' mandate to act and act quickly is an unambiguous one, the principals have no clear mandate. Their power stands in delicate balance: If they delegate too much authority to their teachers, they are seen as ineffectual and lacking in vision. If they do not delegate enough authority, they are seen as tyrannical. If the teaching staff is mostly tenured, the principals wield no actual power over the teachers and cannot use fear to motivate. Nor, lacking discretionary funds for the support of exceptional staff projects or for rewarding outstanding performance, can they use the incentive of money.

Research on school principals has shown them (like teachers) to be conservative and oriented to the present.[7] Their concerns are understandably with maintaining a cheerful status quo, avoiding crises, and attending to problems as they arise. Tenured, and with no imperative to make change, the principals' success in their jobs is most frequently gauged by their ability to keep peace and avoid the unexpected.

The differences between the preoccupations of the principal and those of the superintendent were well illustrated in the early planning meetings of Quest. From the start, it was clear that the superintendent wanted a new program in place as soon as possible. Cara Miller saw the teachers' reticence to move quickly as a rationalization based on fear: "Change is always scary for people. I've never found people totally ready to plunge in." Her job, she claimed, was to give the teachers the necessary "nudge off the side of the pool." Miller's impatience for change came through clearly in the very first planning meeting she attended, when she urged teachers with great insistence not to worry about the schedule, the union, and other serious uncertainties that rightly preoccupied them. Indeed, teachers' fears were well-founded. Not only did the rushed entry into implementation produce the very problems the teachers had predicted, but Miller herself left the district by the end of the following year.

The principal, on the other hand, projected a dramatically different affect from the central administrator. At meetings, Fitzgerald's answers to the teachers' questions were invariably circumspect. He would "do what he could," he could "promise nothing with 100% certainty." Fitzgerald's position toward the design of Quest was clearly a complicated and uncomfortable one. On the one hand, he was obliged to support his boss (whose enthusiasm for change demanded acknowledgment and action). At the same time, he was the one responsible for actually creating the desired schedule and for placating the other teachers who were not receiving release time. If the program failed, it would be Fitzgerald's "neck in the noose," not Miller's. The superintendent would blame him; the teachers would blame him. In short, his reticence was understandable.

The Consultants

As anyone who has ever been a public-school teacher can testify, few individuals are so subject to ridicule and loathing and so vulnerable to the labels of nuisance and buffoon as are the educational consultants. What public-school teacher, at the sound of a consultants' opening remarks, has not opened a knitting bag or exhumed a folder of papers to grade? The roles of teachers and consultants seem, by their very definitions, to be antagonistic. The teachers dwell, by necessity, in the realm of the practical and the immediate. No matter how drawn they may be to the theoretical, the teachers are still engaged in what is essentially a hands-on, product-oriented task, full of concrete expectations and concerns. The consultants (especially the staff-development professionals) breathe a more refined air. As sympathetic as they may be to the arduous reality of classroom life, their loyalties are first and foremost to the series of theoretical principles that they want the school or teacher to adopt. Indeed, their livelihoods are dependent on the success of that adoption. The livelihood of teachers, on the other hand, is in no way linked to any kind of specific program success. And, given the vicissitudes of a teacher's day, new program implementation is necessarily a low priority. Hence, the natural enmity between the two.

College consultants (e.g., Ed Smith and I) are a hybrid of the teacher and the staff-development professional. We hold no fierce loyalty to an ideological program, and we have no overt pecuniary stake in promoting change. Indeed, we were as skeptical of prepackaged reform as the teachers. And yet, unlike the teachers, we believed in the efficacy of theory and research to solve educational problems. Situated as we were in the middle ground between ideology and practice, we would seem to have been a useful partner for the high school. Armed with an established body of research to guide teachers' ideas and with no hidden agenda or time frame, we expected an easy, fluid collaboration. Instead, our relationship was fraught from the start with tension; a tension that deepened as the chaotic first year of Quest unfolded.

One of the key problems from the beginning was a lack of definition of our role as collaborators in reform. Much has been written in recent years about the fine distinction between collaboration and cooperation in school-college efforts, with a good deal of literature offering definitions of one and the other.[8] Hoyt (1978) defined *collaboration* as taking joint responsibility and authority for basic policy decision-making. He noted that collaborators share a mutual commitment to one set of goals, with both parties standing to gain in equal measure from the adoption of those goals. Collaboration demands what Hannay and Stevens (1984) called "the bracketing of respective egos," a kind of shared humility in the face of larger purposes.

Cooperation, on the other hand, assumes two distinct and autonomous interests agreeing to work together for mutual benefit. Cooperating parties need not share the same goals, participate in joint policy-making activities, or suffer the same fate. Cooperation is a term that is not particularly in favor in contemporary staff development literature. It describes a relationship that may be seen as old-fashioned in that it is not purely democratic. Parties can cooperate with other parties without necessarily respecting or liking them. Collaboration, on the other hand, assumes both sentiments.

Initially, Blair College defined its role as collaborator in the Quest partnership, similar to many other such partnerships across the country. We threw the term around loosely in the early stages of our work, and we spoke of the founding of the Quest program in plural terms (intended to encompass, in equal measure, the teachers and the college faculty). The motivations that initially brought us into partnership with Brookville High School seemed to mesh well with principles of collaboration. We were there to serve but also to be intellectually challenged and to experience the thrill of seeing innovation take shape. In short, our first, professed goals were the same as those of the teachers.

But with the coming of difficulty, the collaboration began to unravel. Ed and I began to feel that the expertise we did possess went largely unheeded. It was confounding when, weeks into implementation, curriculum seemed to be the last item on anyone's agenda. Talk of logistics and classroom management couldn't hold Ed's interest, and it was not for such talk that he had entered into the partnership. Having no real ties or obligations to the enterprise, he gradually pulled back from the fray.

Ironically, the glue that continued to bind Blair College to Brookville High School was of a mercenary variety—the desire on my part to write a book on the Quest program. My desire to gather data, to have free access to the Quest class and the privilege of interviewing students, kept me bound to the teachers even through their most difficult months. Such a motive for participation on my part clearly moved our relationship from a textbook definition of collaboration to a cooperative endeavor. And yet, without the goal of data collection, my own interest and investment would frankly have waned, as did Ed's. In short, both sides had to be getting something concrete out of the relationship.

In many ways, the relationship between the Brookville faculty and the Blair consultants improved once Blair took a step back from the work of

Quest and defined its relationship to the program in less intimate terms. Ironically, for so-called collaborators, the relationship between the teachers and the college faculty felt less equal. Ever present in early planning sessions, the college consultants were invariably treated as experts. No matter how much we tried to give the floor to our colleagues from the high school, our supposed power and expertise invariably gave us the last word. Teachers would often proffer suggestions with their eyes trained on Ed or me, as if our facial expressions could belie the efficacy of their ideas. Although neither Ed nor I were privy to any special information, we were treated at certain early points as if we held the answer to a mystery and had consciously chosen to mete it out as slowly as possible. As described in the narrative, the college faculty had the power in such meetings to completely derail a mood or a discussion with a single question or a disapproving look.

The inequality of our early collaborative relationship became painfully apparent when things started to go wrong. Although we had, early on, enjoyed some degree of veneration, we were nonetheless perceived as outsiders and encumbrances in times of great difficulty. Our own decision to stand back in such instances (explained later in more detail) was a perfect indication of our true relationship to the work at hand: There were clear and certain limits to our investment.

After a year of implementation, I believe the teachers of Quest came to see Blair faculty for what we were, well-meaning individuals who held few answers to many of the real problems encountered in the reform process. Demystified in this way, we could begin to repair our damaged relationship. We attended only those meetings to which we were invited; we responded to specific calls for help (generally by finding source material or gathering assessment information on students); and we interceded with the principal and superintendent on behalf of the teachers. These kinds of functions were helpful and well within the limits of our ability. In return—and the reciprocal aspect was crucial to the equality of our relationship—I felt welcomed into the Quest class as a researcher. In short, both sides seemed to learn the lessons of a good therapy session: to lower their expectations of others, and to forgive themselves.

The Inevitable Gulf Between Theory and Practice

As suggested above, all too frequently during the planning and teaching phases of the Quest program, Ed and I felt helpless to address problems. When interpersonal tensions flared, when student misbehavior became overwhelming, and when time constraints made meaningful talk impossible, my presence in the group seemed mortifying. What advice could a college consultant possibly give? What research-based strategies would alleviate squabbling between two ideologically opposed teachers? So much of what thwarted the successful design and implementation of Quest in its first years had little to do with research-based principles. Indeed, one often felt more acutely the need for a priest than an educational expert.

Ed and I first reacted to the "spiritual" problems of reform by focusing on what we knew. "Curriculum," we insisted, "is the key to resolving difficulties." If teachers would simply focus their energies on refining the troubled curriculum, then their other problems would resolve themselves. Advice of this sort may be sound in the abstract, but it takes into account not at all the human realities of the change process, nor the complexities of school life. Gail, Bill, and the other first-year Quest teachers could no sooner have focused on curriculum than they could cease to argue among themselves.

Indeed, in the first 2 years of collaboration, our work was rife with examples of *cultural clashing*. The most blatant of these clashes took place around language problems. Each constituency (college and high school) spoke its own distinct tongue and had difficulty interpreting the language of the other. Predictably, the language of the college contingent tended to be theoretical; the language of the high school teachers, practical and concrete. Ed would insist on the use of certain terminology (the distinction, for example, between skills and concepts) to an audience of teachers who saw little relevance in the distinction. To them, outcomes were either positive or negative, regardless of what you called them. The teachers' interest in, and insistence upon, spending their planning time on the nitty-gritty of classroom organization confounded the college consultants. As outsiders, not involved in the daily work of teaching, we tended to underestimate the importance of such work.

Outside Consultants

In addition to Ed and myself, a third and larger consulting agency for Quest was the Coalition of Essential Schools organization. At least four times in 2 years, individuals or groups representing the Coalition came to give information, advice, or support.

In certain ways, the Coalition consultants were at a distinct advantage. Blair, by downplaying the value of their own and others' opinions and by calling on the teachers to find answers in themselves, had worked to establish a relationship of equals. The Coalition consultants, however, came with no pretense of equality: They were experts with a clear agenda. They carried the weight and prestige of Sizer's Coalition with them. In many ways, the Coalition consultants resembled the traditional in-service trainer of the sixties: Their visits were one-shot, and their recommendations were founded upon a series of predesigned principles. They observed the chaos of the first year Quest class in operation, offered euphemistic praise (e.g., "The students seem so comfortable with you!") and a few suggestions, and then left. Much to my annoyance, the teachers of Quest seemed to regard the words of the Coalition consultants as gospel. The visitors' praise was discussed and repeated with a relish that was almost unseemly; their suggestions were adopted immediately and without question. The effect of this on me, as the "local consultant," was similar to the effect of one's spouse too lavishly praising the spouse of another person. My tendency was to find fault whenever possible in the suggestions, comportment, or affect of these presumptuous outsiders.

In reality, however, the interplay between the internal and external consultants was a healthful one for Quest, a point reinforced in a number of large-scale studies of staff development.[9] The Coalition visitors brought with them a necessary infusion of glamour, as well as a sense that something big and powerful was backing the Brookville reform work. Some of the visitors (especially Bob McCarthy) genuinely inspired the faculty to lend a more sympathetic ear to the reform agenda. I believe my own role was far less glamorous, but also important. After the first turbulent year of implementation, Blair had become a predictable, supportive presence and a voice of advocacy.

Notes

1. In his seminal study of teacher attitudes, Dan Lortie (1975) considers the *psychic* rewards and liabilities of the job. Those teachers who experience few psychic rewards (e.g., positive feedback from students, a sense of purposefulness, collegiality) tend to burn out at a much faster rate. Indeed, the majority of teachers in Lortie's study placed psychic rewards above other kinds (e.g., extrinsic rewards) in terms of desirability. More recent studies of teacher attrition corroborate Lortie's findings. Aram Ayalon's (1989) study, "Predictors of Beginning Teacher Burnout," surveyed 45 first-year teachers concerning role overload, instructional rewards, job design, role ambiguity, classroom environment, goal clarity, and frequency of interactions with other teachers and administrators. The study

found that positive recognition and adequate time for planning and instruction were critical in reducing teacher burnout. Also relevant is Barbara Heyns's (1988) follow-up of a national longitudinal survey analyzing characteristics of career teachers.

2. For a broader discussion of the importance of teacher collaboration, see Susan Rosenholtz (1985).

3. The isolation of "reform-minded" faculty from other teachers in the school is a phenomenon that is often mentioned in discussions of small-scale or incremental reform efforts. Coalition researchers D. E. Muncey and P. J. McQuillan (1991) see this bifurcation as an inevitable characteristic of the reform process.

4. In a series of studies conducted in 40 classrooms at two high schools over the course of 3 years, Fullan and Eastabrook (1973) concluded that the predominant orientation of students bound for college or university was to cover the course topics and to get good grades.

5. In interviews, a random sample of Quest students were asked to explain or assess various aspects of the class that reflected its larger program goals. Students were questioned twice, once at the start of the year, and then again in April. A sample of the questions and the responses from three students (identified as A, B, and C) follows:

Q: What are two ways in which working in groups is different from working independently?

October:

A: You get more answers to the question, and it's a little easier because there are more people.
B: You don't have to do all the work yourself.
C: When you work in groups, you're supposed to cooperate.

April:

A: One is that you can ask people what to do. The other is that it's better because you get to share ideas.
B: You get the opinion of other people. If you're stuck, you can turn to someone and ask their views or whatever. If you have a big project and only half the people do any work, then you don't have cooperation and it's hard to get anything done.

C: You can't do whatever you want. You can't say, "I'm gonna do this," because other people will say, "No, I want to do that." I found I like working by myself. Someone might change or throw away what you've done, and that's frustrating.

Q: Tell me three things you like about working in groups.

October:

A: I don't like anything about it.

B: One of your friends might be in the group. It's easier—too easy. There's less pressure.

C: You get to talk more about stuff with your friends. It's easier.

April:

A: One is, I like to talk with them. Two is, the more I work with people the more I get to know them—their personalities and stuff. It's nice getting to know more people.

B: It's easier when you work in groups to come up with interesting topics. You get more input on what you say.

C: I like all the ideas you get. You say one thing, and you get all these ideas. You say one thing and maybe two other people will agree, and it gets better and better. You get more creative.

Q: What are two things you have learned in Quest that help you in your other classes?

October:

A: I don't know that I've learned anything in Quest. It's basically time and space occupation. It fills third and fourth periods.

B: Listening a little harder. Because in this class you can't understand stuff because there are so many people talking.

C: How to work in groups better.

April:

A: When I read, I understand more. I learned to read all different kinds of things.

B: To work well with people. To communicate better.

C: Research skills. I learned to go to the library and look up things, and I actually know what I'm doing. When I go to the library, I'm not intimidated. I learned about zoning, and that has helped me in my civics class . . . and about revenue, a topic I just had to write a paper on for civics.

We concluded from these interviews that students tended to value and assimilate interpersonal lessons above all others.

6. During the 1980s, dozens of large-scale studies considered the central role of the principal in reform. Several of the more comprehensive studies are those by Barth (1990), Fullan (1988), Hall and Hord (1987), Leithwood and Steinbach (1989), and Smith and Andrews (1989). These studies focused on a range of principal and reform issues including ideal characteristics of the reform-minded principal.

7. Sarason (1982) and Lortie (1987) claim that the conservative tendencies of the principal have historical roots. Both scholars conclude that characteristics of the traditional bureaucratic system of public schooling tend to isolate principals. Lortie notes that principals who challenge the status quo are more likely to agitate both conservative parents and resistant teachers. He sees this as a logical disincentive to reform.

8. For examples of the ongoing debate on the subject of collaboration and cooperation, see Clark (1988), Hord (1986), and Townscend (1992).

9. For a lengthy discussion of differing roles of internal and external consultants and their relationships to one another, see Fullan (1991).

8

Understanding the Nature of School Change

Three years of work with the Quest Program have changed the way I think about school reform. As a participant observer throughout Quest's ordeal, I have come to question many of the easy assumptions I held upon entering our partnership. Schooled in the literature of reform, I had carried with me ideas about process, pacing, and funding needs that ultimately were shown to bear little relation to reality. Virtually none of the treatises and texts I had studied in preparation for my work with Brookville High School prepared me for the complexity of institutional change, nor did they offer concrete suggestions for ameliorating the many difficulties encountered.

What follows are six basic understandings about school reform that have replaced for me the preconceptions with which I began. The understandings refer to a range of issues and dilemmas which repeatedly presented themselves throughout our work. I believe these lessons apply in some measure to all schools engaged in the arduous process of reform.

The Critical Importance of Funding

There has been much debate in recent years among school reformers about the efficacy of starting small versus starting big. Should schools approach change through a series of quiet, incremental transformations (i.e., the classroom-by-classroom approach), or should institutions seek instead to remake themselves through radical, comprehensive reorganization? The arguments in support of each approach are numerous and pervasive. Those who advocate the small change approach argue:

1. The effects of such changes tend to last longer.
2. There is less risk taking, and hence less chance of failure.
3. Faculties are more willing to buy into changes that disrupt the status quo only minimally.
4. In every respect, the change process is easier to oversee and implement.

Those, like Theodore Sizer, who advocate large-scale restructuring argue the opposite:

1. Small changes tend to become diluted and disappear.
2. The absence of risk becomes synonymous with low-commitment. Risk demands a level of investment that energizes the risk taker.
3. Faculty becomes bifurcated and contentious when reforms are implemented by only small fractions of the teaching staff. Conversely, large-scale change creates a solidarity of purpose, a vital sense that we are "all in the great experiment together."

Finally, proponents of large-scale change argue that the sorry conditions of schools demand dramatic action, not tinkering. However, to debate the merits of either approach (large or small) in an abstract context is to ignore the key issue in school reform: the fact that change is contingent on money. The degree of change, its persistence and scope, must be tied to the budgetary realities of a community. Even with a motivated faculty, meaningful reform involves expense (for release time, for new materials, for training, for redefining teachers' jobs, and for ongoing staff development).

Those who downplay the critical importance of funding (from Bill Clinton to Ted Sizer) are simply ignoring the real complexity of the task at hand. Certainly, there are teachers who will adopt innovations and take on extra work without additional compensation. Certainly, there are teachers whose minds are so astute and flexible that they can easily integrate new ideas and approaches without ongoing staff-development support. But, there are other teachers (probably more) who will habitually resist change or whose intentions are good, but whose capacity to understand the new is limited. These teachers can also be brought on board—but at a price. Without sufficient expenditure of funds, the restructured school will find itself with a new form but no new function, a restructured version of the status quo.

Money is essential. Even small changes require some financial backing. Quest's arduous first year would have been eased by additional money for release time, by compensation for teachers doing a sixth class, by funds for new materials, and by additional personnel to take over "duty" assignments. The absence of this support led to circumstances so demoralizing that they caused one talented teacher to leave the field altogether and others to back away from innovation, seeing it as an overwhelming and exhausting enterprise. How presumptuous then to believe that the full faculty at Brookville High School could be made to buy in to reform, without an additional penny being spent on their behalf. The notion is simply absurd.

In a recent article in *Harper's* magazine, sociologist Benjamin Barber (1993) eviscerates both taxpayers and policymakers for their hypocritical complaints about schools:

> Most educators . . . agree that although money can't by itself solve problems, without money few problems can be solved. Money can't win wars and put men in space, but it is the crucial facilitator. It is also how America has traditionally announced, "We are serious about this!" To me, the conclusion is inescapable: we are not serious. We have given up on public schools. (pp. 45-46)

As long as local, state, and national agencies refuse to adequately fund school change, it will be hard to believe that anyone is really serious about reform.

A Balance of Centralized and Decentralized Power

The last decade of school change literature has increasingly advocated decentralization as the vital key to lasting reform. The evils of centralization have become part of the unquestioned liturgy of reform: Centralization breeds an unhealthy standardization; it undermines the significance of the teacher's knowledge; it reinforces antiquated power relationships. The appeal of a decentralized approach is readily apparent. In a decentralized system, principals or teachers, or both, initiate, design, and implement programs precisely tailored to the needs and politics of their own school culture. Authentic site-based control of reform initiatives offers teachers an opportunity to move beyond the tedium of classroom instruction and to experience the empowerment of self-rule.

However, decentralization in theory and in practice are not necessarily the same. Studies of school-based initiatives (including a range of site-based management initiatives) conducted in the last 5 years confirm the great difficulty of sustaining a genuinely decentralized system. Levine and Eubanks (1989) have identified six obstacles to school-based models of empowerment:

- Inadequate time, training, and technical assistance
- Difficulties of stimulating consideration and adaptation of inconvenient changes
- Unresolved issues involving administrative leadership on the one hand and enhanced power among other participants on the other
- Constraints on teacher participation in decision making
- Reluctance of administrators on all levels to give up traditional prerogatives
- Restrictions imposed by the school board, state and federal regulations, and by contracts and agreements with teacher organizations

As the story of Quest illustrates, Brookville High School was profoundly encumbered by all six of these obstacles. First, the reform efforts at the high school were thwarted by a lack of release time and by ineffective support from the administration and the college collaborators. Second, the overall faculty of the high school remained, at least in the first years, largely unmoved by the curricular initiatives of the Quest teachers. Third, the principal's role and his level of support were unclear to the teachers, and that uncertainty tended to irritate existing problems within the experimental program. Fourth, scheduling problems and a general failure to focus constrained teacher participation in decision making. Fifth, the principal's tendency to overburden teachers with the minutia of running their own program distracted them from the difficult work of curriculum design. And, finally, a general lack of financial support on the state and local levels meant that Quest teachers had to work on a shoestring budget and largely fend for themselves.

One of the critical lessons of Quest is the need for a more realistic balance between centralized and decentralized control of change. Indeed, the assets of centralized initiatives have been long overlooked because of a blanket assumption that decisions made outside the school are all brutish mandates, insensitive to the unique properties of individual schools. The central administration in Brookville was hardly out of touch with the needs and concerns of teachers. They were fully abreast of the struggle experienced by the Quest staff, and they were genuinely sympathetic to the teacher's plight. On frequent occasions, Cara Miller admitted to Blair faculty her concerns for the teachers, bemoaning the fact that they were overworked and burdened by the poorly constructed schedule. But, nonetheless, the administrators persisted in doing little or nothing to direct or resuscitate the failing program. The Quest teachers consistently felt the profound drawbacks of absolute school-based control: isolation and abandonment, a lack of focus, and a confusion about their place in the larger initiatives in the school. The laissez-faire attitude of the central administrators was interpreted not as freedom, but as rejection. Especially in times of difficulty, Quest teachers looked to the superintendent for direction, resources, and feedback. Too frequently, they received only a generic nod of support or an occasional commendation for their hard work and perseverance.

Quest's experience with the state education office seems to illustrate even more dramatically all that is most problematic with the existing norms of power and control. The state of Massachusetts had recently embraced the principles of the Coalition of Essential Schools to the extent of setting up a state office for support and dissemination of Coalition principles. The Quest teachers quickly affiliated with this state office, looking to it for financial support and help with staff development, which was unavailable on the local level. Representatives from the state office visited the school once or twice; several Brookville High School faculty were invited to number of workshops around the state; the school was given a small grant for use in educating the faculty at large about the Coalition principles. In return, Brookville High was required to reach consensus as a full faculty about becoming a Coalition School by the end of their second year of exploration. Otherwise, no future funding from the Coalition office would be made available.

Clearly, given the complex reality of Brookville's faculty, such a consensus was impossible to reach in so short a time. Indeed, as the Quest teachers pointed out to the state representative, Sizer himself had claimed that the process takes 5 years if it is to be done with integrity and any hope of maintaining lasting effects. Yet, the state stubbornly insisted that the school was in charge of its own fate: Brookville High had been given the freedom to change and had failed to meet the challenge. No money would be forthcoming for the following year.

Decentralized or site-based initiatives for change too often emerge as punitive exercises for those bold enough to rise to their challenge. Simply because teachers have taken it upon themselves to identify problems and initiate solutions, they cannot, therefore, be expected to follow through alone with implementing and sustaining those programs. If administrators support the development of grass roots initiatives (as so many claim to do), they must be ready to offer real and palpable help once those initiatives get underway.

Which aspects of the reform process should be centralized and which decentralized? For the Quest program, the delineation was absolutely clear. Ideally, the tasks of each constituency would break down as follows:

Decentralized Tasks

- Performing needs assessments
- Developing general strategies for addressing identified needs
- Identifying personnel to implement those strategies
- Implementation

Centralized Tasks

- Providing financial assistance at all stages of reform
- Providing resources and expertise as needed
- Evaluating the effectiveness of new strategies
- "Selling" successful new programs to the community

The survival of Quest after 3 years of implementation has little to do with the support or services received on the district or state levels. As with many grassroots change efforts, the teachers performed most of these centralized and decentralized tasks themselves.

Working With the Faculty You Have

As the story of Quest makes manifest, the great strength of the program, as it finally emerged, was in its capacity to promote self-esteem, public-speaking skills, positive group dynamics, and independence. Less successful were the academic aspects of the curriculum—the push for critical thinking and rigorous independent research. Students formed extraordinary bonds of friendship and developed a rare tolerance for their peers, but the quality of the work they produced was more pedestrian. Certainly, bright students did outstanding projects. But, ultimately, most students performed at predictable levels. The Quest experience may have helped children develop essential social skills, but it did not (for the most part) transform academically weak students into stronger ones.

To a large extent, I believe that the outcomes of Quest are a direct reflection of the talents and strengths of its teachers. Although curricular "softness" in the first year could clearly be blamed on logistical problems (e.g., the lack of shared planning periods, the unwieldy team structure), those problems were largely ameliorated by the third year of implementation. Yet, in the third year, the focus of growth was still on the affective, rather than the cognitive. The curriculum continued to lack the high rigor it had initially been designed to promote.

Clearly, once inhibiting factors have been removed, one must look to the teachers for the source of any program's strengths or weaknesses. The great talents of Bill, Sue, and Ellie were in their ability to mold and socialize a disparate, difficult group of young people; to move beyond differences and prejudices and create a warm, creative environment for learning. Their own personal warmth, fair-mindedness, and genuine love of adolescents created a world in Quest that was, like them, warm, fair-minded, and loving. Although their desire to promote high academic standards was sincere, they were not able to achieve a high level of intellectual rigor in the class. Despite the particulars of the curriculum or the prodding of the Blair consultants, the Quest teachers intuitively returned to their own strengths in the classroom; emphasizing the affective over the cognitive.

Good teachers are good in many different ways. No staff-development workshops or reform mandates can dramatically change the essential personalities and talents of faculty. Rational, well-funded innovations can develop teacher strengths and diminish teacher weaknesses, but no program can transform a teacher into something entirely new. A program cannot create an intellectual, or turn a martinet into a sensitive, caring individual.

Reformers need to realize the supremacy of innate teacher characteristics in their work with schools. Personality and native talent take precedence over even the most powerful of ideologies or the most compelling new piece of equipment. It is the given, the immovable starting point. Ignoring the reality of who your staff are may produce an illusion of short-term gains: Individuals can be intimidated into mouthing virtually anything under duress. But, in classrooms, teachers revert to their true selves. Good reforms tap into the best of what teachers have to offer; in Quest's case, three fine sensibilities. Bad reform simply engrafts change onto hostile tissue. Inevitably, the organism will reject it.

Using Broad and Patient Assessments

Was Quest a "successful" reform? It depends on what and how you measure. Obviously, the success of any curricular reform must be gauged in some measure by learning outcomes. But, as the previous passages have asserted, learning outcomes themselves can be broadly defined. Attitudes toward school, toward the self, and toward the concept of lifelong learning are all outcomes that are difficult to measure and even more difficult to prove to skeptical taxpayers concerned with the bottom line.

Yet, even if the learning outcomes for Quest are neutral, there are other equally critical measures of success to be found in changed *teacher* attitudes and skills. Programs like Quest, which tap into teachers' needs for collegiality and feedback, have a real and measurable impact on a school's overall effectiveness. Reform, when it is done right, increases productivity, energy, and enthusiasm. The teachers teach better, not only in their new, experimental classes, but also in their regular classes. The Quest teachers spoke often about learnings that "transfer" to classes outside of Quest. Quest has served then as an antidote to burnout; a massive injection of adrenaline in the 20th mile of the marathon.

Unlike a decade ago, when rapid teacher attrition caused a steady influx of new blood, teachers in the nineties are resisting retirement in increasing numbers. Economic uncertainty and the modest rise in teachers salaries are keeping potential retirees in the field longer than ever. Clearly, as the teaching force ages, strategies will be needed to prevent these veterans from stagnating. Bill, Ellie, Sue, and Jan offer clear evidence that reform can not only take hold among veteran teachers, but that it can act as a transfusion for them. Thus, in assessing change in schools, researchers need to look more closely at teachers, and the powerful impact of attitude changes on productivity, enthusiasm, and commitment.

The Limits of Collaboration

Perhaps the most far-reaching of the lessons learned from the Quest experience concern the realistic limits of collaboration. In Chapter 7, I discussed in detail the apparent limits of college consultants' aid and commitment, and I argued for a less romanticized, more needs-bound relationship between schools and colleges. Earlier in this chapter, I discussed the limits of collaboration in teaching: Too complex an interdisciplinary collaboration creates scheduling and logistical problems that distract teachers from the pleasures of teaming. Also, too many personalities interacting together set up the kind of internecine feuding that almost destroyed the program in its first year of implementation.

Yet, another aspect of collaboration, which came under scrutiny in our work, was in the area of curriculum design. The teachers and Blair faculty, like many other similar partnership teams, began their curriculum work excited by the notion of democratic composition (i.e., the collaborative design of an interdisciplinary course). But, the reality of collaborative work of this nature fell far short of our imagined ideal. Little of intellectual substance was produced during our all-day planning sessions as participants squabbled over minute details or moved in distracted tangents from the topic at hand.

It seems that the inevitable stumbling block to collaborative curriculum design is the human ego. With each small curriculum decision subject to democratic vote, participants (myself included) seemed incapable of holding back their own two cents. Every philosophical notion or fleeting ideological bugaboo came onto the table to be argued and discussed. What was more, the curriculum work offered fertile ground for playing out issues of power and control that had been more successfully repressed up to that point. In so obsessively democratic an environment, power inevitably became an obsession.

Ultimately, finding itself mired in democracy, the group stumbled its way back to traditional methods of composition. Although each individual participant composed several pages of the curriculum, Bill culled the work, made the final choices about what would be included, and then typed the document itself. Similarly, in the first year of implementation, collaborative decision making about how to teach the curriculum proved impossible. By the end of the third month, Bill was making all decisions himself and running the teamed class like a traditional teacher and five "aides" to help him out.

Indeed, at virtually every stage of Quest's life, collaboration or innovation has given way to conventional work structures, with participants calling the experimental format too unwieldy, impractical, or confusing. The shift after the first year to a smaller team of three and a less and less integrated curriculum is yet another example of this *drift toward tradition.*

As a consultant whose conception of reform was initially derived from journals and not practical experience, I was annoyed and disappointed at this tendency toward the status quo. But, I believe now that it is an inevitable and healthy response to the arduous realities of reform efforts such as the ones described in this book. With virtually no support or compensation for its efforts, how could the group be reasonably expected to continue a structure and format that required excessive work and received little positive feedback from either students or parents?

The Failure of Theory

For more than 3 years, I have watched the faculty at Brookville High School debate, discuss, and dissect the goals, philosophies, and beliefs that they hoped would come to undergird their reform efforts. They have engaged in these discussions as a full faculty, raising their voices in cavernous cafeterias. They have also formed countless study groups, focus groups, councils, and committees to discuss their ideas more intimately. Visitors from the State Board of Education have led teachers and parents in a "visioning session." Teachers have attended workshops for developing "purposes" and "intentions" for the school. Yet, all of this rhetoric of theory and all of this abstract talk of goals have produced virtually nothing to improve the daily working conditions of the average teacher. Indeed, the endless theoretical conversations have become yet another burden for the vast majority of Brookville teachers— taking up precious work time on the rare curriculum days when faculty might be grading papers or organizing materials.

Even the Quest Program itself owes little to theory. The terrible lethargy that bogged down the early curriculum-design sessions at Blair College can be traced to a misguided notion that a fleshed out theoretical system must serve as the preliminary foundation for all curriculum decisions. Teachers struggled to articulate a cognitive framework for their course, stumbling over the obscure language of theory only to quickly abandon that curriculum once they entered the classroom. There they reverted to familiar, practical strategies disconnected to any theories of cognition.

Generations of academics have bemoaned the apparent gulf between theory and practice, placing the blame for that gulf largely on the shoulders of teachers. Teachers, it is generally believed, are either unaware of theory or else too lazy or too overworked to apply it in their classrooms. If only teachers would integrate theory in their work, we academics sigh, then the quality of instruction would be greatly improved, and schools would be more unified and purposeful.

Working with Quest, however, I have come to believe that this habitual abandonment of theory is not the teachers' fault. Nor is it the fault of theory, which is often both provocative and potentially useful. Rather, I believe that we underestimate the immense gulf between the two realms. We assume that there is some direct link between abstractions and actions, a link which teachers, were they sufficiently attentive, would recognize and act upon.

Instead, there appears to be a terrible void, a kind of Bermuda Triangle, between reform theory and practice. After each tortuous faculty dialogue on philosophy and goals, teachers mutter: "Where do we go from here?" and "What's next?" Theoretical talk makes action feel much more overwhelming. As a result, I have come to believe that, at least for school change, the direction of theory and practice must be reversed. Instead of saying, "Here is an appealing theory of change; let's try to implement it;" a faculty would be better served by saying, "This is a problem I have in my class; this is a solution I'd like to try. Has anyone tried it before? What can I learn from their experience?"

Far more useful to the Brookville teachers than all the workshops, committees, and discussion sessions were their visits to other schools engaged in similar reform efforts. Such a visit inspired Bill's initial ideas for Quest itself, and subsequent visits served to console and inspire the struggling teachers at various points in the implementation process. Never once did I hear teachers refer gratuitously to a theoretical reading they had done. Yet, the stories of other schools' triumphs and difficulties were constantly being told. Indeed, they became a kind of spoken liturgy, sustaining Quest in its darkest moments.

This book represents an attempt to put that liturgy into writing. The literature on school change has, for too long, failed to provide the kind of practical resources teachers and administrators need in order to persist with reform. Those practical resources are not theoretical scaffolds or stories of change that excise complication and failure. They are plainspoken, realistic models of how innovation takes root in schools. Site-based reformers would do well with a whole database full of such models, each presenting the story of a unique institution struggling in unique ways. The problems, resolutions, and compromises of such institutions would provide a true and thorough education in reform; an education far more valuable than whitewashed case studies and ideological rhetoric. These real and candid models are the best guide and the best medicine for an enterprise that is, even *with* that support, extraordinarily complex and difficult.

Moving Toward a Change: A History
Brookville High School

Spring of 1990

The superintendent, principal, and a team of teachers spend a release day in discussion with Blair College faculty members. The topic revolves around a proposed mentor program with Blair interns to include a minority outreach on the part of Blair to recruit candidates for its graduate program in education.

Several faculty members attend a conference in Simsbury on the Coalition of Essential Schools.

1990-1991

Initial collaboration with Blair faculty members leads to the formation of a discussion group. About 30 high school faculty members participate in discussions of educational reform, including a review of teaching and learning in general. Readings are made available and become the basis for monthly discussions at Morgan Hall at the college. Discussions become increasingly centered around the Coalition of Essential Schools (CES) and its nine common principles. The group receives release days for visitations and curriculum initiatives. Teachers from Clay (the Coalition school) make a presentation at Blair. Cooperative learning workshops become an ongoing process in Brookville and several high school teachers become involved.

In December, a visitation is made to Andover followed by a visitation to Masconomet Regional.

In January, a visit is made to the Watkinson School and to Narragansett.

In February, a visit is made to Avon. Eight members of the discussion group produce a proposal for a pilot program for grade nine students. It will consist of

40 students, be interdisciplinary, have a team of teachers with common planning time, and use the Coalition's nine common principles as its basis for development.

In February, the pilot program proposal is made to the faculty and is approved by them. The faculty also votes to become an affiliate of the CES as an Exploring School.

In the spring, Brookville attends its first meeting sponsored by the Department of Education to explore change. Appropriated funds are used to develop the pilot program curriculum that was approved by the school committee.

In the summer, Quest teachers complete training in cooperative learning strategies. Interested faculty members continue reading including *Horace's Compromise* (Sizer, 1984), *A Place Called School* (Goodlad, 1984), and *High School* (Boyer, 1983).

1991-1992

The Quest pilot program gets underway with eight teachers participating in various roles and two acting as anchor teachers. Meetings with Quest parents are held, and students present a final exhibition at the end of the year. An evaluation of the program occurs, and a decision is made for its continuance. A visitation is made to Hope High School.

Cooperative-learning workshops continue to be offered. A Brookville team consisting of the principal and teachers attend Department of Education training sessions and network with other specific CES schools in the process.

Throughout the summer, some faculty members continue reading *Horace's School.*

1992-1993

Brookville receives a $5000 grant as an Exploring School. Quest continues with three anchor teachers, and another teacher joins during common planning time. The whole faculty works on Goal Committees for the year exploring curriculum, study skills, technology, school governance, scheduling, assessment, and the CES.

In October, a teacher attends the first meeting of the New England Coalition Network. Local networks are established. A team of two teachers from Brookville join the Connecticut Valley Coalition Network until a larger group can be formed in the area. The CES group in the school, numbering about 20 members, continues discussions and receives several visits from Department of Education representatives for these discussions.

Visitations are made in October to Fenway Middle College High School, in November to Falmouth, in January to Mt. Everett, in March to King Middle

School, and in April to Nobel High School. Eight teachers use a release day to review where they have been and to make recommendations. These include enhancing communication with the whole faculty regarding the common principles, expanding the Quest program in grades 9 and 10, obtaining financial support for Quest planning, obtaining support for those interested in developing interdisciplinary courses, and encouraging and supporting for those interested in looking at alternative scheduling models.

In January, Robert McCarthy of the CES makes a presentation to the whole faculty.

In February, the faculty is presented with the recommendations of the release day participants. It supports the expansion of Quest and the other recommendations. In the spring, cooperative-learning workshops continue with about 30 high school teachers attending. The school committee approves expanding Quest in grade 9 to include 80 students and adding a Quest II in grade 10 for 40 students. The faculty invites parents to participate in a "visioning" exercise, and at the April Parent-Teacher Organization meeting, approximately 70 parents and teachers participate, led by Barbara Sengi of the Department of Education.

In May, with Barbara Sengi facilitating, the whole faculty begins the process of visioning to consider what a student from Brookville High School should know and be able to do upon graduation. This is the first step toward reaching a consensus on learning outcomes, and it will proceed next year to closure.

Also in May, five students and two faculty members take part in a 2-day conference at the University of Hartford as part of the New England Coalition network. They engage in visioning exercises. The five Quest teachers for 1993-1994 apply for summer curriculum work time. The Principal and team of five teachers apply to attend TREK (a retreat for teachers and administrators in Coalition Exploring Schools) for a week in the summer to learn about development of an action plan.

In June, the union calls for work-to-rule slowdown.

1993-1994

The third year of Quest begins in September with two sections of freshman Quest and one section of sophomore Quest.

Quest Curriculum: Year 1

Composed by Ten Teachers From Brookville High School With the Support and Collaboration of the Blair College Department of Education and Child Study

Preface

The educational aims embedded in the curriculum that follows represent the tangible realizations of more than a year's thinking, planning, and organizing by a group of Brookville High School teachers and Blair College faculty members. Meeting informally in the summer of 1990, the group initiated a series of discussions focused on public school reform and, in particular, Ted Sizer's compelling arguments for curricular and structural changes. The Quest program is the outgrowth of those early, provocative discussions.

Although it is relatively easy to condemn the structural rigidity that characterizes most American high schools, it is a more formidable matter to shape viable alternatives to that kind of endemic, institutional self-compliance into which schools seem to have slipped. School reform is, not surprisingly, a complex elusive and often frustrating task. That the commitment to such reform moved beyond simple discussion to a programmatic implementation of a pilot course bent on fundamental curricular change is a tribute to the high school faculty, Brookville's supportive school administration, Blair College faculty members, and, most important, the enthusiastic parental encouragement.

The Quest curriculum is perhaps best described as not so much a tightly prescriptive, content laden "subject" to be covered and absorbed by students over a year's time, but as a series of thematically related activities that call for students to confront certain assumptions, pose hard questions about those assumptions, and engage in assignments that often call for crossing conventional curriculum boundaries. In essence, the Quest program lays out a process and set of questions that open up the possibility of different perspectives and multiple responses. It is, we think, a curriculum that challenges and sharpens rather than regulates thinking.

The Quest program is untested at this writing. Nonetheless, it has, by its very emergence, demonstrated the productive possibilities of reshaping the educational imperatives of a public enterprise in whose health teachers, administrators and parents all have a common stake.

QUEST PLANNERS
AUGUST, 1991

Change:
Essential Questions

What is change?

What causes change?

Which changes are natural and which are man-made?

What are the effects of change?

When is change good? Bad?

Is change predictable?

How is change affected by choice?

How do I deal with changes I don't choose?

What helps us adapt to change?

Can I affect change?

Unit 1: Personal Change

Introduction to team, course, and expectations. How is this course different from others? Essential questions and overall philosophy, who makes the rules, and how. Communication games (e.g., Zooley, logic puzzles) to orient students to working in groups.

Then: What are the essential questions connected to personal change? This will be explored through individual journal writings and then shared in small groups and finally as a large group. Ideas will go up on the blackboard or poster paper. From there, the class will group ideas into three main areas of interest: physical, intellectual, and social change. Other questions that may surface and can be tied into the unit/course as we go along may include, Are there observable patterns to test changes? Do we have control over these changes? What is technology and how does it affect us?

Explore physical change in the following series of interconnected activities. For homework, find a baby or other early photo of yourself (teachers included) and also ask your family for information about your earliest self as others remember you. For example, where and when were you born, who was present, what was your birth weight and length? Were there any birthmarks? Were there birth problems (e.g., preemie)? Who were the first people to learn of your arrival? Are there any funny stories about this period?

Then, after posing your photo and possible bio sheet, see how many can guess who is who. Who has changed the most and least? Post a current Polaroid snapshot beside each baby photo. Make a list or write an essay about all the ways you have changed physically in the last 14 years. Which changes do you like and dislike?

A biology teacher or pediatrician could instruct students about a variety of topics, for example, how an embryo develops, how the body changes in 14 years, and in what ways or in which years do we change the most physically?

Explore social change using the microfiche collections of the *Hampshire Gazette* at our library and *Forbes,* research newspaper headlines and front-page stories for each student's birth date, first day of school, and each subsequent fifth year (e.g., 1977, 1982, 1987, 1991). Students should also check national news magazines for those years. This research would be an ongoing out of class project taking perhaps 2 weeks for everyone to get to a microfiche reader. Finally, each student would create a collage on poster board of events, dates, and major changes occurring on his or her birthday in those particular years. All research notes would be turned in as part of the assignment.

Other social change activities include first brainstorming about what sorts of questions and changes we want to explore. Then, interview each other in pairs to learn about the changes in each other's lives. Over the years, what sorts of changes have there been in friendships, interests (e.g., athletic, intellectual, entertainment), family moves, new schools, and so on? Did these changes affect other changes in a student's life? How would students rate the changes on a scale of 1 to 3 as positive or negative? The end product of this work would be a timeline in which students chart changes in their own lives and perhaps also incorporate the social changes covered earlier.

An additional social change activity is constructing a family tree going as far back as possible to the countries that the students' ancestors came from. Post that information on a world map, and use string and tacks to connect those original countries to Brookville. Some questions to consider: How many of us are native Americans? Native to Brookville? Are there patterns of immigration to Brookville? What sorts of reasons did people have for coming to America and Brookville?

Intellectual, social, physical changes can be studied in an "oral history" project using journal writing, groups, and lectures. An oral historian or reporter may be brought in as a guest speaker. Assign students to interview family members, neighbors, clergy, and others who have known them over the years and who can help students learn about their own lives in the context of changes observed from a variety of perspectives. Students will present an oral or written report (or both). It might be useful to have each report represent two or more different views of the student.

An alternative focus here could be for students to examine when they learned key lessons, knowledge that was important for their development, and who they are today. One way to approach this is by examining their favorite stories (e.g., books, movies, magazines, television shows, fairy tales) singularly or in combinations to explore the range of interests they've had at different periods in their lives. Why were the students attracted to these stories, and what might they have learned from them? A possible guest speaker here might be a professional writer of children's stories or a teller of folk tales.

An ancillary activity here is to read (or have a teacher read to class in a "story hour") *Peter's Pocket*. Have students examine a partner's book bag, locker, and so on to see what "primary artifacts" reveal about a person. What story do such artifacts tell? This might be an appropriate time to have a professional archaeologist from one of the colleges speak about the nature of archeology research.

Have students work on redesigning their room.

Books should be considered for background reading. Students should keep a literary journal, which would be handed in for a grade. Students would be responsible for leading a discussion on their books and addressing certain fundamental questions that stem from the essential questions about personal change that have emerged in the unit. These essential questions may be useful in guiding some of the journal responses. Questions may be given to students when they choose a book, so that questions for each book can be specific to its plot, characterization, and theme.

Possible texts include *A Tree Grows in Brooklyn, A Separate Peace, Diary of Anne Frank, Fences, Odyssey, Red Sky at Morning, Great Expectations, The Chosen, To Kill a Mockingbird, Nigger, Death Be Not Proud, Out of Love, I Know Why the Caged Bird Sings, The Miracle Worker, Nobody's Family Is Going to Change, Works, The Story of My Life, The Yearling, Adventures of Tom Sawyer, Jane Eyre,* and *Lord of the Flies.*

Some of the above works in film or video versions may be shown and compared to the literary work read, especially those stories that examine change.

As a final assignment investigating personal change, have the students write a letter to themselves as a senior. The letters will be saved and returned to students in three years. The letter can address a student's hopes and expectations for his or her high school career. Students should also write a letter stating their goals for this year. These letters will be returned in June. Students can then note if there are any changes in attitudes in the course of a year.

Unit 2: Neighborhood Change

A definition of "neighborhood" is developed by the students, formed into random groups for brainstorming. The concept of a variable is discussed. What are the variables to be considered in defining or characterizing a neighborhood? Students then group the variables into classes or categories (e.g., geographic, social, political, economic) on the blackboard. The class decides on a definition of neighborhood and the variables which affect it. Perhaps at this point, students could research various "planned neighborhoods and cities" (e.g., Levittown, New York; Brazilia, Washington, DC; a Shaker Village, Echo Hill, New Seabury, Cape Cod, and Reston, Virginia). An additional assignment might be to survey television programs for neighborhood settings that impact the show and its concept (e.g., Sesame Street, Cheers). Students would report back to the larger group. This work would be a link to the unit on "Cities," and it may be a more useful activity just before that unit is to begin.

Using the definition of neighborhood is agreed upon and after the research on planned communities has begun, identify an area of Brookville as a possible setting to study.

The students prepare to invite other people from Brookville (e.g., minister, business people, principal, policeman, mail carrier, children, city officials, residents, superintendent of schools) to talk about their ideas of neighborhood in order to appreciate other views of the concept of neighborhood. Students should discuss whom they want to invite and why. They should write a letter of invitation and the letter should describe what the class is doing, why they would like that person to visit, and what they would like the speaker to talk about. Optional dates should be provided. The letter should be followed up by a phone call. A student will introduce invited guests to class. After the presentation students will have a series of questions ready to ask the speakers. In order to prepare for this question and answer period, the students should practice mock appearances beforehand in groups of three. Two students will be interviewer and interviewee, and a third student will take notes during the interview.

Possible readings during this unit include *The Chosen, To Kill a Mockingbird, Romeo and Juliet, West Side Story, Walden Two*, and excerpts (interviews) from *Studs Terkel*.

Each student is given a road map of the city. A large range of map-reading skills are taught (e.g., scales, keys, North-South-East-West, elevation). Exercises include locating certain streets, writing directions from point A to point B, and determining how far to Florence using the scale. This could be independent or group work, and could range from simple exercises to more difficult ones involving topographic maps. A Zoning Department representative should be invited to class to discuss different kinds of maps as well as zoning ordinances.

Students check if their definition of neighborhood has changed as a result of previous activities and speakers. The students should return to their original neighborhood groups where each student in group takes one category by which a neighborhood can be studied (e.g., social, economic, geographic). Students then pair up with students in other groups who have chosen the same category to study. This is a good time for teachers to join each different group. Students then research their categories, after which they bring back findings to their original neighborhood group. This group then puts together a presentation for the whole class that reflects each member's findings.

Suggestions For Research

    Economics. Research census forms, tax records, public assistance, assessed valuations. Create graphs and charts to reflect findings. Bring up concepts such as some things are not in our control; quantitative (numbers) versus qualitative, aesthetics, wealth.

    Politics. Research voting districts. Possibly use councilors as speakers.

    Geography. Have City Planner as speaker. Look at zoning maps. Identify farming and wooded areas. Search for samples of plants, leaves, twigs, and flowers. Catalog these, relating to open spaces and smaller spaces. Include an endangered species list (e.g., ladyslippers). Some more extended activities involving math and science skills might be put into place here.

    Physical. Have architect visit and discuss form versus function. Document social and architectural features. Have students prepare: (a) photo essay—perhaps using black and white film and developed at the high school, (b) technical drawings, (c) artistic rendering, and (d) a video.

During the above activities, students should look at changes over time. Long-time residents may be brought in as speakers.

Students re-evaluate the concept of neighborhood. Perhaps some students may study and research one of the Brookville homes for the elderly (e.g., the history of the house, how it came into being). Students could visit and interview residents of one of the houses (e.g., Lathrop House, Walter Salvo). Students should practice interviewing techniques beforehand (using a video camera) and they should make the arrangements for visits with housing directors. Careful planning before visits is a must. Students should arrange for transportation and visit project extensively, recording on video, and also in notes, what they discover. After interviews, the students could write short stories, plays, and poems using material they have gathered in the activity. A documentary video may be edited for class presentation as well as for presentation to the residents of the visited home during a follow-up visit. Thank-you notes should be sent after the visits.

Another option is looking at other places in the city that have changed (e.g., Main Street). Find photographs of the city throughout the last 10, 20, and 30 years. The plot of the film *Back to the Future* might be used as a motif to present research findings.

Students design a neighborhood. First, students discuss how their concept of neighborhood has changed. What are critical elements to look at when neighborhood is discussed? Design a neighborhood of the future by creating a completely new one or redesigning one that already exists. This can be a neighborhood previously studied or another area of Brookville. Group discussions during this time might include the following questions: Do we need to change at all? What is "outdated?" What is missing? Can one go to "other places" for some things or must they all be in one's neighborhood (e.g., goods, services entertainment)? The designed neighborhood should reflect the activities and skills used in the previous assignments (i.e., use of blueprints, scale models, drawings with labels, maps, plot plans). Students should present to class and parents and should be able to defend their designed neighborhood in a question and answer forum.

Unit 3: City Change

In group discussion, students consider: What is a city? Is it a group of neighborhoods? Does it have a "personality?" Is it a useful scheme for organizing people? What relationships exist or are created among people who live in a city? Are cities necessary? Does my city affect me? How does knowing the city's history help in planning the future—or does it? How and why does a city change? How are those changes measured and documented? Do changes affect the outward appearance of the city? Is Brookville made up of more than one community?

As a large group activity, students create a list of the types of changes that occur in a city. Use newsprint and tape to the wall all the class's suggestions. In smaller groups, categorize changes into major themes. Check with class to see what major themes emerged in the various groups. Each group is assigned or chooses a theme and works on writing the types of information they think should be gathered to measure a change. Students, with the help of teachers, must contact a city agency to get documentation of these changes and graph the information. For each graph, write an explanation of what the graph shows. Within groups, the students should make projections of the possible future of that change with substantiation of their ideas. A presentation to the class will follow. Presentation should include their information, ideas, and city agency contacted. Compile a class directory of agencies for future use.

Individually or in groups, students find old pictures of the city. Students look for or take (using a pinhole camera) photos. The class makes a display of the pictures and determines the major changes and possible reasons for change. If a particular neighborhood has changed, students must redraw a neighborhood map showing that change.

Each student should write a survey designed to get at someone's idea of what a "community" is and how it functions (e.g., What is the community center? In what language does it function? What do those involved get from it? Has the community changed?)

Working in pairs, the students compare their individual surveys and draft a final survey. Students make contact with three people from different races, ethnic groups, cultures, or subcultures and interview them using the survey forms created. Students write a page about the existence of communities in the city and how they have changed, and label any community centers on a map of the city in the room.

Individual journal writing. What kinds of information would it be helpful to have in order to characterize or better characterize Brookville?

Create a diary of someone real or fictional who lived a specific number of years ago (e.g., a student at Brookville High School, Brookville Vocational, Brookville School For Girls, St. Michael's, Brookville Commercial College, Brookville College) and describe a month or year in that person's life in Brookville. Include mention of their family, neighborhood, school, church, downtown, social, athletic, and school activities. This assignment calls for research of the time period chosen.

Pick a year in the past that would allow you to create separate diaries of a student from each of the schools listed above. Compare each one's life for a week.

Choose a person (student or staff member) pictured in an old Brookville High School (BHS) yearbook and recreate their life story as much as possible through research. Use old photographs, tintypes, and things in the Howes Collection at Brookville Historical Society; ads and listings in old copies of the City Directory and telephone books; the Sylvester Judd Collection of journals from 1800-1860; and the microfilm collection of the *Daily Hampshire Gazette* going back to 1796. What can BHS yearbooks tell us about the history of the high school and the city? What can Blair College yearbooks tell us?
   The Brookville Book has numerous articles about city places and people of the past. It can be an invaluable resource text for students engaged in writing assignments that deal with recreation of the past.

Suppose you and your family must move to either Amherst, Brookville, or Easthampton (or any comparative pairing) because your parents have received fantastic job offers in the area. How will you decide which town to live in? Which one is likely to be the best choice for your family? What are your criteria?

Pull together neighborhood data with the data on the business sector to profile the changes in the city over a number of years. Research town reports to catalog changes in city services. Have the changes been good or bad? From whose perspective?

1. Present changes visually through graphs, charts, photos
2. Interview people from major identifiable groups (e.g., the education community, business, ethnic and religious groups). How has change affected the lives of the people involved?
3. How has the work force changed? Can local people find work here? Can employers find a skilled work force? Create graphs, charts, reports to show change.

Have the Zoning Board chairman or building inspector give demonstrations showing what zoning is and how it affects people's activities. What zoning changes have taken place in the city in the last 15 years? Students should find out what type of zoning exists in their neighborhoods and how this affects them.

A categorizing and logic activity. This activity involves students gathering data on a number of places located in Brookville (e.g., restaurants, schools, hotels, stores, streets). The students would then classify the data in some logical way so that a flow chart leading to a computer program of the information would be possible. Essentially the activity would lead students through the steps necessary in creating an *information processing* system.

A second part of the activity would ask students to create a *problem-solving program*. In this project, students would build on paper a decision-making instrument. This would involve working with variables and assigning point values to different variables. The students' ultimate task would be to create a model that would allow a user to feed in certain information and receive an answer to a particular question.

Spanish immigration to Brookville. Research what countries these immigrants came from. Show these countries on a map. Interview at least three people as to why they came to the United States. Invite a speaker to address the class.

Studying change by focusing on an institution. Students are given a choice of several projects which explore historical change. Examples include

City government. As Brookville progressed from a small community to a city, the types of governance changed from small town meetings to a city council of nine members. Students could research when each type of governance was used to run the town, the population at that time, how effective each was, and how the system evolved to what it now is. Students could present a historical town meeting of a particular year, replete with costumes. Students should also attend a current city council meeting and observe parliamentary procedure at work.

School governance. Students can research the development of school committees as the governing body of the school system. What are the reasons for its existence, and the reasons for its existence as compared to more state and federal control? Interview School Committee members as to their views of education. Students might consider devising another system for organizing and governing schools.

Culminating project for the unit—City Predictions. Based on studies done during this unit on city changes, students in small groups will prepare a projection of what the city will be like in 2020. In addition, proposals regarding what institutions (e.g., government, schools, libraries, hospitals) should look like in order to accommodate change will constitute part of the project. Graphs, charts, maps, and drawings, should compose part of the activity. Presentation of the project might be held during the evening with the parents attending.

Unit 4: World Changes

What is our definition of the world? How do we perceive of it? Has it been perceived in other ways? What elements do all nations have in common? Is it useful to see the world as multiple neighborhoods? Are the ways we say boundaries being created by neighborhoods in a city relevant to describing and understanding the world?

What is a culture? Why are there different cultures? Are there rules that define particular cultures? Are we affected by other cultures? What are the rules of our culture?

Begin with the students playing the Alpha-Beta game. What does the game demonstrate about cultures? For a writing assignment, students should detail their observations about what occurred when the game was played.

How have views of the world changed over time? What changes in technology allowed for this change in world views?

Make a map of the world as members of the class know it firsthand. In small groups, interview students and teachers to find out where they have been. Make a map that shows a world composed only of those places. Draw in a different color the places of which the students have "secondhand" knowledge. Write a description of the world in both cases and explain how or if one's views are changed when secondhand information is added. Include in the description the places one is most and least certain of. Does hearing things secondhand affect reliability?

Relate this experience to ways in which first maps were made and to ways they were enhanced as new information became available. What allowed people to travel and get firsthand information? Perhaps an activity that involves research on dried foods for storage, some math on the percentage of water content of foods, fraction of total food weight that actually had to be hauled in travel, ways to get pure water from sea water, and so on might be brought in at this point.

Examine some of the various depictions of the world in use today (e.g., globes, projection maps, Mercator projections, nautical maps, upside-down maps, photos from space). Write a description of the types of information provided by each map and the type of technology necessary to obtain such information. Determine the size of the earth using flat maps and a scale of distance for the globe.

How has technology changed the world? How long has this taken? Find out who invented the street light, train locomotion device, blood plasma storage system, peanut butter, ice cream, plans for Washington D.C., or another invention of student's choice. Research the life of an inventor, exploring such ideas as: Were they "successful?" Did society need what they invented, or did they create a need? Were their ideas ignored at first? How did people accomplish the task performed by this invention prior to its marketing? What are the pros and cons of this invention? These activities might be presented orally.

Think of some device that is "needed." Draw a scale model of the device. Construct a scale model of it (in cardboard or wood). Do a market feasibility survey. Create graphs of the survey information (i.e., plot age or sex of respondents and their receptivity to the device). Research how to obtain a patent on a device. Prepare a market strategy to sell the device. Examine how television and print ads sell a product. Using what you have discovered, develop a television ad and a magazine layout for the device.

A final paper and oral report to class will conclude the activity. What are the differences between inventing and marketing some new device today versus the experiences of the inventor researched earlier?

Has technology made our world smaller? List how different parts of the world are connected and draw them on a world map. Include cross-oceanic telephone cables, and major air and sea routes. The list may include natural connections, such as wind and water currents. Be prepared to tell which are a cause of new technologies.

Explore how many other cultures you are in contact with daily. Research the cultural origins of objects you have touched, food you've eaten, sport teams you've watched on television, places you've read about in the paper, and people you have spoken with. What were the technologies that brought each of these to us?

Research the origins of your families. Put pins and strings on a wall map to show how "we" came to Brookville. By what technologies did we arrive?

Be a travel agent and plan a trip around the world with sightseeing stops on each continent. Plan the route. Over what countries will you fly? Are there countries that must be flown around? What differences would you expect to find between each continent or country? What denominations of money will be needed in each country, and how much of each currency will you need? What are the exchange rates? Does one need visas? What are U.S. relations with each country visited? Book your flights and list departure and arrival times. How many time zones will be crossed? How many miles will be traveled in all? Invite a professional agent to speak to the class.

Can we create a miniature version of the earth? Read articles on Biosphere II and view the accompanying videotape. List what you would put into an ecosystem. Build a terrarium out of a soda bottle, collecting as many things on your list as you can find and fit them into the bottle. Decide where and how this ecosystem must be kept so that it will last for the year.

Does ecological change in one part of the world affect the rest of the globe? Can one person affect changes? Research some major world event, such as the Mount Saint Helens eruption, Chernoble, destruction of the rain forest in Brazil, coal burning or sulfur dioxide production in some part of the world, the Valdez oil spill, and oil drilling on the coast of Scotland. Look for effects on other parts of the world. Are there any? Look for evidence of individuals making a difference in this area. Look in newspapers for information on global environmental change. Make a collage of clippings. Photocopies of the articles placed on the collage should be kept under separate cover. These will be presented in small groups and exhibited in classroom. Students must look at all exhibits and keep a log of common themes and stories that seem exceptional.

Choose one environmental change on which to become an expert. Research the causes, possible effects of change. Put research findings into book form, including graphs, charts, and drawings.

Research an animal that is endangered. This must include writing for information from Greenpeace or World Wildlife Fund. Write a descriptive essay based on your findings and theorize how the world would be different without that animal.

As a culminating class project, students might compile a book about ecological changes and place the book in the library. In addition to expository articles, the book might include art work and fictional pieces as well as graphs, charts, tables, and maps demonstrating a variety of ways to represent change.

Unit 5: Changes in the Universe

What is our sense of "the universe?" Have there been historical changes in the way we perceive of the universe? How did these changes emerge? Is our view of the universe in the process of changing even now? Does scientific thinking change social thinking or does social change precede changes in scientific thinking?

Assign groups to research areas of scientific thinking about the universe from Copernicus to modern day. Some groups may wish to study the mathematical component of science's changing perceptions, while, at the same time, other groups may wish to focus on the social conditions that affected (or were affected by) changing scientific views. Some crucial questions will probably arise in this unit: Have scientific developments allowed us to control change or do they have a life of their own that leads to further discoveries and subsequent social change? Is anyone in control? Has scientific development brought the world together or has it created conflict?

Field trip to Platt Museum planetarium and observatory.

Charting the changing relationships among sun-moon-earth. Students keep track of and draw pictures of how the moon appears every night. This information is kept on a chart. Compare students' charts of the moon.

 For a demonstration in class, assign someone to represent the sun (using a flashlight), someone to act as the moon (using tennis ball), and someone to represent the earth (using basketball or globe). In the darkened room, experiment with positioning of the earth, moon, and sun to recreate some of the phases of the moon. A recorder's job is to compare the results of this activity with charts drawn earlier. How do the results of this demonstration compare with what students know about the movement of celestial bodies?

Look at tide tables and compare with the lunar calendar for the same time period. Write a paragraph about observed correlations, and create some kind of graph that will display the relationship between lunar movement and tides.

Seasonally, interview at least three different classmates on their ideas about why seasons change. Working with a partner, compile the results of the interviews. Tally the number of people with similar responses. Compare tallies across groups. Research the actual reasons for seasonal changes, first by studying diagrams of the earth's orbit, tilt, and rotation. Present your thinking in small groups.

Learn to use a star wheel. Predict the constellations that will be seen in Brookville on a particular night. Check the prediction by drawing what you see that night.

Create a fictional log of travel to a celestial body. Read a Native American folk tale about the origin of a particular constellation and then write one of your own creation myths.

If one could send a message into outer space in Morse code, what message would be sent? As a supplementary assignment some students may wish to learn Morse code, build a model of the instrument, and "send" their messages to other students who act as receivers from another star.

Research a particular planet. Using know environmental factors of that planet, create a "life form" and culture consistent with known factors. Present your created society through a prepared skit or some other fictional genre.

UFO debate. After researching the claims and counterclaims of those who have written about the subject, the class will set up a debate on the resolution: There is life outside the planet earth.

Future studies. Speakers from several area colleges will address this topic. Predictive sorts of activities may from the basis for assignments as a culmination for this unit.

RESOURCE C

Quest Curriculum: Year 2

Law Segment

Part I: Explanation of the Project

At the end of this unit of study and research, you and your partners will have to take the stand in front of a panel made up of a teacher, a lawyer and a parent from this class. You and your partners must be able to answer any one of the following essential questions based on your readings from the information in this packet.

You and your group must also be ready to present your Creative and Research projects.

Each member of the group must hand in a position paper based upon the selections presented on this paper. If you wish to come up with a different topic to take a position on, please consult with me (Ms. Polaski) prior to the actual writing.

Part II: Essential Questions

1. What is law?
2. Does a society need laws?
3. What makes a good law?
4. Where did our laws come from?
5. What are the classifications of law?
6. How do cases proceed through civil courts?
7. How do cases proceed through criminal courts?
8. Be prepared to discuss the judicial process.

Part III: Take a Position

Do you agree or disagree? Defend your position.

Each member of the group must select a *different* question. This is an individual grade.

1. The strongest society is that society that has the most laws.
2. Nazi Germany had laws. Would you have obeyed them if you had lived there?
3. Does the state have the right to enforce all laws?
4. Of the four characteristics usually found in a good law, which one is the most important. Why?
5. Are parole and probation useful or dangerous ways of dealing with law-breakers?
6. What arguments can you make for and against the position taken in the Massachusetts constitution that the best means of protecting citizens from abusive government is by a combination of *representation, separation of powers, checks, and balances?*

Part IV: Research Projects

Select two research projects.

1. Who are the Supreme Court justices? Find a picture and give a brief biography of each one.
2. What is the right to habeas corpus? Explain why it is one of the most important protections of individual freedom.
3. Discuss a historical case from the city of Brookville.

Timeline for the In-Class Assignments

Wednesday 10/28

Read pages 399-403. Do the section entitled "In Review." Hand in one paper per group with all names by the end of class.

Thursday 10/29

Read pages 403-406. Do the section entitled "In Review." Hand in one paper per group with all names by the end of class.

Friday 10/30

Read pages 406-410. Do the section entitled "In Review." Hand in one paper per group with all names by the end of class.

Monday 11/2

Read pages 410-413. Do the section entitled "In Review." Hand in one paper per group with all names by the end of class.

Tuesday 11/3 and Wednesday 11/4

Read the Summary section on page 414. Do the sections entitled "Using Vocabulary" (on page 414), "Review Facts" (on page 415), and "Building Skills."

You and your partners will discuss how to go about distributing the work. By the end of the second day you will finalize your answers and hand in one paper with the names of all group members on it.

Thursday 11/5

You and your partners will discuss any of the Essential Questions to this chapter to make sure you all have an understanding of the information. Remember you will all be responsible to one another when you are before the panel. You will all have to speak. Help one another out.

Friday 11/6

Work on another segment to this project, whether it be the research topics or creative topics.

Final Exhibition Evaluation Sheet

Group Criteria

Distinguished

1. Evidence of cooperation with members in group
2. Everyone in the group understands all the material
3. Much respect is shown toward group members and to invited guests
4. Presentation and appearance of material is well organized and effective
5. Responses to all questions are well thought out

Satisfactory

1. *Some* evidence of cooperation with members in group
2. *Some* members in the group understand *some* components of material
3. *Some* respect is shown toward group members and to invited guests
4. Presentation and appearance of material is organized and *somewhat* effective
5. Responses to questions are *somewhat* thought out

Unsatisfactory

1. *Little* evidence of cooperation with members in group
2. Members in the group *do not* understand any components of material
3. *No* respect is evident
4. Presentation and appearance are unorganized and ineffective
5. Responses to questions are *not* thought out

Individual Criteria

Distinguished

1. Presentation is clear, thoughtful, and effective
2. Student speaks persuasively and acts with confidence
3. Work shows creativity
4. Evidence of extra effort
5. Student handles questioning with ease
6. All components for the exhibition are completed
7. Student writes effectively with clarity using appropriate language, grammar, and structure
8. There is total understanding of the purpose of the exhibition

Satisfactory

1. Presentation is *somewhat* clear, thoughtful, and effective
2. Student speaks with some persuasion and acts with *some* confidence
3. Work shows *some* creativity
4. Evidence of *some* extra effort
5. Student handles questioning with *some* difficulty
6. *Some* components for the exhibition are completed
7. Student writes *somewhat* effectively, using appropriate language and minimal errors in grammar and structure
8. There is *some* understanding of the purpose of the exhibition

Unsatisfactory

1. Presentation is unclear, *not* thoughtful, and has *little* effort
2. Student hesitates to speak and lacks confidence
3. *Lack* of creativity
4. *No* evidence of effort
5. Student does *not* respond when questioned
6. Many components for the exhibition are missing
7. Student writes with *no* clarity using inappropriate language with major errors in grammar and structure
8. There is *no* understanding of the purpose of the exhibition

RESOURCE E

The Common Principles
of the Coalition of Essential Schools
by Theodore Sizer (1984, 1992)

1. The school should focus on helping adolescents learn to use their minds well. Schools should not attempt to be "comprehensive" at the expense of the school's central intellectual purpose.

2. The school's goal should be simple; that each student master a limited number of essential skills and areas of knowledge. These skills and areas will, to varying degrees, reflect the traditional academic disciplines. However, the program's design should be shaped by the intellectual and imaginative powers and competencies that students need, rather than by "subjects" as conventionally defined. The aphorism "less is more" should dominate. Curricular decisions should be guided by the aim of thorough student mastery and achievement rather than by an effort to merely cover content.

3. The school's goals should apply to all students, although the means to these goals will vary, as students themselves vary. School practice should be tailor-made to meet the needs of every group or class of adolescents.

4. Teaching and learning should be personalized to the maximum feasible extent. Efforts should be directed toward the goal that no teacher will have direct responsibility for more than 80 students. To capitalize on this personalization, decisions about the details of the course of study, the use of students' and teachers' time, and the choice of teaching materials and specific pedagogies must be unreservedly placed in the hands of the principal and staff.

5. The governing practical metaphor of the school should be *student-as-worker* rather than the more familiar metaphor of *teacher-as-deliverer-of-*

instructional-services. Accordingly, coaching will be a prominent pedagogy in order to provoke students to learn how to learn and thus to teach themselves.

6. Students entering secondary school studies must demonstrate competence in language and elementary mathematics. Students of high school age who have not yet achieved appropriate levels of competence for entering secondary school studies will be provided with intensive remedial work in order to assist them to quickly meet these standards. The diploma should be awarded upon a successful final demonstration of mastery for graduation—an "exhibition." This exhibition by the student of his or her grasp of the central skills and knowledge of the school's program may be jointly administered by the faculty and by higher authorities. Because the diploma is awarded when earned, the school's program proceeds without strict age grading and without any system of "credits earned by time spent" in class. The emphasis is on the students' demonstrations that they can do important things.

7. The tone of school should explicitly and self-consciously stress the values of unanxious expectation (e.g., "I won't threaten you but I expect much of you"), trust (until abused), and decency (i.e., fairness, generosity, and tolerance). Incentives appropriate to the school's particular students and teachers should be emphasized, and parents should be treated as essential collaborators.

8. The principal and teachers should perceive themselves first as generalists (i.e., teachers and scholars of general education) and second as specialists (i.e., experts in one particular discipline). Staff should expect multiple obligations (e.g., teacher, counselor, manager) and should feel a sense of commitment to the entire school.

9. In addition to total student loads per teacher not exceeding 80 pupils, ultimate administrative and budget targets should include substantial time for collective planning by teachers, competitive salaries for staff, and an ultimate per pupil cost not to exceed that at traditional schools by more than 10%. To accomplish this, administrative plans may have to show the phased reduction or elimination of some services now provided students in many traditional, comprehensive secondary schools.

References

Adler, M. (1982). *The Paideia proposal: An educational manifesto.* New York: Macmillan.

Ayalon, A. (1989, April). *Predictors of beginning teacher burnout.* Paper presented at the meeting of the American Educational Research Association, San Francisco, CA.

Barber, B. (1993, November). America skips school. *Harpers, 287,* 39-47.

Barth, R. (1990). *Improving schools from within: Teachers, parents, and principals can make a difference.* San Francisco: Jossey-Bass.

Boyer, E. L. (1983). *High school: A report on secondary education in America.* New York: Harper & Row.

Carroll, J. M. (1990). The Copernican plan: Restructuring the American high school. *Phi Delta Kappan, 71,* 358-365.

Chira, S. (1991, May 4). Money's role questioned in schools debate. *New York Times,* p. 1.

Clark, R. W. (1988). School university relations: An interpretive review. In K. Sirotnik & J. Goodlad (Eds.), *School-university partnerships in action: Concepts, cases, and concerns* (pp. 32-67). New York: Teachers College Press.

Cogan, M. L. (1976). Educational innovation: Educational wasteland. *Theory Into Practice, 15,* 220-227.

Donovan, J. F. (1992). The Hunter model: A four year longitudinal study of staff development effects. *Journal of Research and Development in Education, 25,* 165-172.

Doyle, W. (1983). Academic work. *Review of Educational Research, 53,* 159-200.

Foley, F. J. (1976). The failure of reform: Community control and the Philadelphia public schools. *Urban Education, 10,* 389-414.

Fullan, M. (1988). *What's worth fighting for in the principalship: Strategies for taking charge in the elementary school principalship.* Toronto, Canada: Ontario Public School Teachers' Federation.

Fullan, M. (Ed.). (1991). *The new meaning of educational change.* New York: Teachers College Press.

Fullan, M., & Eastabrook, G. (1973). *School change project.* Unpublished manuscript, Institute for Studies in Education, Toronto, Canada.

Goodlad, J. I. (1984). *A place called school: Prospects for the future.* New York: McGraw-Hill.

Goodlad, J. I. (1990). *Teachers for our nation's schools.* San Francisco: Jossey-Bass.

Gursky, D. (1991). Madeline! *Teacher Magazine, 3*(2), 28-23.

Grant, G. (1988). *The world we created at Hamilton High.* Cambridge, MA: Harvard University Press.

Hall, G. E., & Hord, S. M. (1987). *Change in schools: Facilitating the process.* Albany: State University of New York Press.

Hannay, L. M., & Stevens, K. W. (1984, April). *The principal's world: A case study of collaborative research.* Paper presented at the meeting of the American Educational Research Association, New York.

Hargreaves, A., & Dawes, R. (1989, April). *Coaching as unreflective practice: Contrived collegiality of collaborative culture.* Paper presented at the American Educational Research Association meeting, Boston.

Heyns, B. (1988). Educational defectors: A first look at teacher attrition in the NLS-72. *Educational Researcher, 17*(3), 24-32.

Holmes Group. (1990). *Tomorrow's schools: Principles for the design of professional development schools.* East Lansing, MI: Author.

Hord, S. M. (1986). A synthesis of research on organizational collaboration. *Educational Leadership, 43,* 22-26.

Hoyt, K. (1978). *A concept of collaboration in career education.* Washington, DC: Government Printing Office.

Hunter, M. (1991). Generic lesson design. *Science Teacher, 58*(7), 26-28.

Kozuch, J. A. (1979). Implementing and educational innovation. *High School Journal, 62,* 223-231.

Leithwood, K., & Steinbach, R. (1989, April). *A comparison of processes used by principals in solving problems individually and in groups.* Paper presented at the meeting of the Canadian Association for the Study of Educational Administration, Boston.

Levine, D., & Eubanks, E. (1989). *Site-based management: Engine for reform or pipedream? Problems, pitfalls, and prerequisites for success in site-based management.* Manuscript submitted for publication.

Lightfoot, S. L. (1983). *The good high school.* New York: Basic Books.

Lortie, D. (1975). *School teacher: A sociological study.* Chicago: University of Chicago Press.

Lortie, D. (1987). Built in tendencies towards stabilizing the principal's role. *Journal of Research and Development in Education, 22*(1), 80-90.

Merina, A. (1993, October). When bad things happen to good ideas. *New England Association Report, 12*(3), 4-5.

Miles, M. (1980). School innovation from the ground up: Some dilemmas. *New York University Education Quarterly, 11*(2), 2-9.

Muncey, D. E., & McQuillan, P. J. (1991). *Some observations on the possibility of major restructuring in American schools: An ethnographic perspective.* Paper presented at the workshop for the School Ethnographic Project, Brown University, Providence, RI.

New England Association of Schools and Colleges. (1990). *Report of the Visiting Committee.* Northhampton, MA: Northampton High School.

Palonsky, S. (1986). *900 shows a year: Looking at teaching from the teacher's side of the desk.* New York: Random House.

RAND Corporation. (1977). *Federal programs supporting educational change.* Santa Monica, CA: Author.

Rosenholtz, S. (1985). *Needed resolves for educational research.* Washington, DC: National Center for Educational Statistics.

Sarason, S. (1982). *The culture of school and the problem of change.* Boston: Allyn & Bacon.

Sarason, S. (1990). *The predictable failure of school reform.* San Francisco: Jossey-Bass.

Shanker, A. (1990). The end of the traditional model of schooling—and a proposal for using incentives to restructure our public schools. *Phi Delta Kappan, 71*, 344-357.

Sizer, T. (1984). *Horace's compromise: The dilemma of the American high school.* Boston: Houghton Mifflin.

Sizer, T. (1992). *Horace's school: Redesigning the American School.* Boston: Houghton Mifflin

Smith, W. F., & Andrews, R. L. (1989). *Instructional leadership: How principals make a difference.* Alexandria, VA: Association for Supervision and Curriculum Development.

Townscend, R. (1992, May). *From isolation to collaboration: An organizational perspective.* Paper presented at the meeting of the New England Educational Research Organization, Portsmouth, NH.

Waller, W. (1932). *The sociology of teaching.* New York: Russell & Russell.

Warren, D. (1990). Rites of passage: On the history of educational reform in the United States. In J. Murphy (Ed.), *The educational reform movement of the 1980's: Perspectives and cases* (pp. 57-81). Berkeley, CA: McCutchan.

Index